GCSE BITESIZE revision

be

499

BBC

Every effort has been made to trace the copyright holders of the material used in this book. If, however, any omissions have been made, we would be happy to rectify this. Please contact us at the address below.

How to Vote leaflet courtesy of HMSO; Castle definition courtesy of Macmillan; Keep Teeth Healthy text courtesy of National Dairy Council; Jazzie B, Queen, 71, Hitting Out, Hi-tech, low-life articles courtesy of Guardian Newspapers Ltd; Easy Pickings and Alarms articles courtesy of Which? Magazine; Is it fair to put Mum in a home? article courtesy of Woman Magazine; Toaster safeguards courtesy of Kenwood; She's Old Enough To Look After Her Own Smile advert courtesy of Greater Mcr. East Education & Training Consortium; RSPCA adverts courtesy of RSPCA; Savoury Eggs recipe taken from Student Grub, pub Clarion Press courtesy of Jan Arkless; Action For Blind People letter courtesy of Action for Blind People; Oxfam advert courtesy of Oxfam; Wild Refuge, How Green Are You?, Beat the Bugs, Water Saving Ideas, Dear BBC Veg Good Food, Green Cleaning articles courtesy of BBC Vegetarian Good Food Magazine; Rhino Adoption Papers courtesy of WWF; Adopt a Humpback Whale courtesy of International Wildlife Coalition Trust; Ninja Peril, Smoking: Ban It In Public Places?, Fireworks: time for a total ban?, Quiet Please, Driving the limit down, courtesy of Manchester Evening News; Tomatoes E. Coli advert courtesy of Milton Fluid; Bicycles cartoon strip taken from How Things Began courtesy of Usborne Books; What Makes a Good Friend?, Teenage Gambling articles taken from Issues 2, courtesy of Collins Educational; Albert Docks leaflet courtesy of Liverpool Tourist Information; Stamp Out Bullying letter, Kaylee article courtesy of Mail on Sunday; Quarry Bank Mill leaflet courtesy of Quarry Bank Mill; Talking to Young People about Alcohol leaflet courtesy of Health Education Authority; Wheels are a Wonder courtesy of Mountain Biking UK; Gee, Mom article courtesy of Daily Mail; Balance of Playground Power courtesy of The Listener.

Photograph p67 courtesy of Luke Finn; p69 courtesy of Oxfam.

Line drawings by Malena Stojic.

Published by BBC Educational Publishing,
BBC White City, 201 Wood Lane, London W12 7TS
First published 1998
© Trevor Ganson, Imelda Pilgrim and Marian Slee/BBC Education 1998

ISBN: 0563 461187

Designed by Malena Stojic
Printed by Bell & Bain Ltd, Glasgow

English

Trevor Gamson
(Senior Examiner GCSE English and English Literature)

Imelda Pilgrim
(Principal Examiner GCSE English)

Marian Slee
(Assistant Principal Examiner GCSE English)
with additional research by Belinda Schofield

Contents

Bitesize English: Non-fiction texts

About BITESIZEenglish

BITESIZEenglish has been designed specially to help you with you GCSE exams. It's not just a book - you can use the TV programmes, too, and you can even access the on-line service where you'll find more activities and an option to e-mail questions to teachers who will help.

You can use the book on its own, but you'll get more out of it if you tape the TV programmes and use them on video as part of your revision plan.

It's called BITESIZEenglish because it's packaged together in small chunks to help you to revise. Most people find it's MUCH easier and more effective to revise a bit at a time and not to try to do everything at once. Bitesize helps you to do this because you can watch, say, around 15 minutes of TV, then read and do the activities on the relevant pages of the book, and you'll have spent perhaps 45 minutes working and will have covered a whole topic. You can watch the video whenever it suits you and as often as you want – it's a good idea to go over anything difficult more than once – then turn to the small section in the book.

If you get stuck or are unsure of something, you can ask your teacher or turn to the on-line team to answer your questions.

KEY TO SYMBOLS

📺 A link to the video

❓ Something to think about

◎ An activity to do

Bitesize doesn't cover everything you need to know, or all the things you'll need to be able to do, but it concentrates on the essentials. If you've worked your way through this book, and watched and understood the videos, you'll have made a really good start. The only thing you may have to check with your teacher is if there are extra areas (eg different poems) that you need to revise; or, indeed, areas such as poetry of World War I that you don't need to revise. We hope Bitesize will give you a head start with your revision and help you to stay in control!

About this book

This BITESIZEenglish book is divided into two main sections – literary texts and non-fiction.

The section on literary texts first looks at the Shakespeare play, Macbeth, and takes you through five key themes in the play. Depending on which exam board you school has entered you for, you might be studying Macbeth as part of your coursework rather than for the exam, but the video and book will still be useful in helping you to understand the play.

There are three sections on poetry which look at poems by William Blake, Seamus Heaney and some of the poetry written around the time of World

War I. In each of these we look at different ways that the poets use language to help the reader to understand what they are trying to say.

The second half of the book is about working with non-fiction text. It is divided into Reading and Writing. You won't find any material on the TV programme about this part but you can find lots of extra material by l ooking at newspapers, magazines and other printed matter. Practise as much as you can and you'll soon notice an improvement in your reading and writing skills.

How this book works

Each section has activities to help you stop and think as you're reading, with some practice questions at the end. Try and answer the questions as if you were in an exam – write your answer carefully and don't let yourself get distracted.

There are lots of reminders to help you as you work through the book – read the Remembers carefully and try and use the suggestions. You may find it useful to jot notes in the margins on some pages – this is your book.

There is also a glossary at the end of the book. This has some of the most useful words you will need for the exam. Make sure you understand all of these words and try to use them in your answers to impress the examiner.

The answers we have given are just suggestions – in most of your answers in the English exam you are asked to give your point of view (whether it's on Macbeth or a newspaper article) and then to support your view with evidence from the text. The success of your answer will depend on how well you can do this.

THE ON-LINE SERVICE
You can find extra support, tips and answers to your exam queries on the BITESIZE internet site. The address is http://www.bbc.co.uk/ education/revision

Planning your revision

Usually students who get the best grades have planned their revision and not tried to cram it all in at the last minute!

Make sure you know the date of your exam and which day each paper is on. Hopefully, you'll have finished your coursework on time and won't have to worry about it.

Think about how much time – realistically – you can spend each day and each week on revision. Don't forget that it's not just English you have to revise!

You may decide to start revision around three months before the exam, in March. This gives you plenty of time so you can use the book two pages at a time, with the video, then perhaps whizz through again in the two or three weeks just before the big day. You may find that you work well spending a couple of hours at a time, so you could work through half of one of the poetry sections in a sitting, with the video. Don't just revise something once

– go back to it after an hour, then a day, then a week if you can. This way, you'll become more familiar with the material and more confident.

Draw up a revision timetable for the days and weeks leading up to the exam, for all your subjects – and stick to it!

When you sit down to start work make sure that:

- it's quiet

- you've got everything you need in the room – pens, paper, TV/video, books and perhaps a dictionary

- you don't get distracted by the telephone, computer games or music

- you don't work for too long without a short break – nobody can concentrate properly for very long stretches, so make sure you set yourself a time limit to keep yourself fresh and alert.

On the day

Make sure you know what day the exam is, what time it is and where it is. If you are allowed to take books into the exam, don't forget your copy – check with your teacher. Get to the exam room in plenty of time and on your way to the exam, go through some of the most important points – you won't learn anything new at this late stage, but you can get yourself into the right frame of mind!

In the exam, check how many questions you need to answer and whether you have any choices to make. You can work out roughly how long each question should take, so try not to spend more time on one answer because you will have to rush something else. Always read the questions slowly and carefully, then plan your answer by making a few rough notes.

Check that your handwriting is clear so that the examiner can read it – you may have written a top grade answer, but if the examiner can't read your writing, you won't get the marks!

Writing for GCSE English

During your GCSE English course, you will be asked to do a number of writing tasks. These have been grouped into four main areas:

- writing to explore, entertain and imagine

- writing to argue, persuade and instruct

- writing to inform, explain and describe

- writing to analyse, review, and comment

Where you do each type of writing depends on the examination syllabus you are following. The table on the next page shows the way each board sets the writing tasks:

Writing type	NEAB	SEG	MEG	EdExcel	WUJC
Explore etc.	Coursework	Coursework	Coursework	Coursework	Paper 1
Argue etc.	Paper 1	Papers 1/2	Papers 1-4	Papers 3/5	Paper 2
Inform etc.	Paper 2	Coursework	Coursework	Papers 2/4	Paper 2
Analyse etc.	Coursework	Paper 2	Coursework	Papers 3/5	Paper 2

There are some skills which you will need whatever type of writing you are doing. These are:

planning your work

This is vitally important, because it shows the examiner that you have thought through the whole piece, rather than just making it up as you go along. The person who marks your work will be looking for evidence that your writing is deliberate. A plan shows that you have thought about:

- your introduction and conclusion
- what each paragraph will be about
- the shape of the writing – the order of your paragraphs

checking your work

When you have finished writing, you must go back and check everything. Look at how your sentences work – are there some which could be clearer? Think about ways you could make your writing more effective by adding or deleting a few words. Look for common spelling and punctuation mistakes – try to be aware of those you often make.

Whatever board you do, it is essential that you know what is distinct about each type of writing you are going to tackle. **BITESIZEenglish** concentrates on writing to Argue, Persuade and Instruct. This is the only group which is assessed by final examination by all five boards in England and Wales. You will need to do further revision on the other types of writing set by your exam board.

We hope you enjoy working with BITESIZEenglish. Now read on...

Good luck!

Literary texts

As you read the chapters on literary texts you will come across several important pieces of information. These concern the authors' lives, the times in which they lived and the influences on their writing. Not every chapter puts equal emphasis on this background information. Some authors were influenced more than others by the times in which they lived. In an examination you are not required to write essays about the life of an author or the sociological background. You do, however, need to be aware of the extent to which outside factors have affected an author's work.

Background knowledge of the First World War, for example, will help you to understand Owen's poetry. In a discussion of "Dulce Et Decorum Est" a brief reference to, say, the number of casualties at the Somme would be enough to show the cause of Owen's bitterness. There is no need to give a detailed account of the fighting.

In each chapter you will find some consideration of meaning, themes, use of language, and the importance of sound and tone. You will find that these topics are not treated in isolation. Examiners would expect you to relate poetic technique to ideas in the writing.

When answering examination questions, you will be required to present your material effectively.

Follow these key steps:

- read the question carefully
- look for the key word or words that tell you what to do
- underline these words.

For example, take this question:

> By examining the language of "The Early Purges" by Seamus Heaney, show how successfully the poet presents his argument.

There are at least two things to bear in mind when preparing your answer to this question:

- the main emphasis of the question is on the **language**, not the content of the poem
- there is a right way and a wrong way of working out the degree of success

In order to decide how successful Heaney is, you must analyse the ways in which he uses language. Do not feel you have to make an instant decision.

First find examples of language use. Then make notes on their effect.

When you come to write your answer, always use the formula: PQD.

- P stands for the **POINT** you wish to make

- Q stands for **QUOTATION**

- D stands for **DEVELOPMENT** of the point.

If you use this formula, it will prevent you from repeating yourself. In answer to this question a weak candidate might write:

> *In this poem Heaney uses the language of real people.* (a good point to make) *He writes as people talk.* (repetition)

> *It's just like people you meet everyday.* (more repetition)

> *As I said earlier, these people in his poems just talk like real people.* (candidate going round in circles)

At this point the examiner realises that he is marking the paper of a weak candidate.

Another candidate might begin his or her answer in the same way:

> *In this poem Heaney uses the language of real people.*

then immediately given a supporting quotation:

> *Dan Taggart refers to the kittens as "the scraggy wee shits".*

then gone on to develop the quotation thus:

> *By referring to the kittens as "shits" Taggart seems to have no feeling towards them. They are something to be got rid of. On the other hand, he describes them as being "wee" which suggests some kind of pity, as in the phrase "poor wee things." Perhaps Taggart is torn between his duty to rid the farm of unnecessary cats and his liking for them.*

This would form the basis of a good essay, because, by using the PQD formula, the candidate is able to advance the argument. The examiner will be able to reward a candidate who shows real understanding both of the poem and the right way to tackle an examination question.

⊡ The witches

When Shakespeare was writing, most people believed in witches. There were regular witch-hunts to get rid of their "evil influence". Many innocent women were accused of being witches and burnt at the stake.

◉ *Read Act 1, scenes i and iii.*

Finding the meaning

When you study the witches in Macbeth, you need to think about what impression they make on the audience and the influence they have on Macbeth.

REMEMBER Use a dictionary to look up any words you're not sure about.

Creating atmosphere

In the short opening scene the witches talk of a battle being lost and won, of a future meeting with Macbeth and their response to familiar spirits (Graymalkin and Paddock). In themselves, these subjects are neither frightening nor disturbing. But think about *how* the witches speak.

Contradictions

The witches speak in verse. Their lines sound like chants. They speak in riddles and paradoxes, for example, "Fair is foul and foul is fair."

This contradiction is echoed by Macbeth when he appears in Act 1, scene i:

So foul and fair a day I have not seen.

REMEMBER Try to notice themes and symbols running through the play.

These contradictions introduce a feeling of opposing forces at war. They are a symbol of the struggles that take place in the play.

Foreboding

The witches create an atmosphere of foreboding. They meet in "thunder, lightning, or in rain". The air is not only "foggy" but "filthy". In just a few lines Shakespeare has managed to create a feeling of anticipation. The audience wonders how the witches' prophecies will be borne out.

⑦ *How would you produce the opening scene of Macbeth so that it had a strong impact on an audience? You should think about the appearance of the witches, the way they say their lines and the background setting, lighting and sound.*

Forces of evil

Do the witches represent evil? Look at the spells at the opening of Act 1, scene iii. The Second Witch has been "killing swine". The First Witch holds "a pilot's thumb". The evil isn't always explicit. Can you feel a sense of menace in the picture of "a sailor's wife" who "munch'd, and munch'd and munch'd"? Look how Shakespeare presents disturbing details. For example, the First Witch will change into a rat with no tail, and ominously repeats "I'll do, I'll do and I'll do".

The witches are powerful enough to control the weather ("I'll give thee a wind") and they hint at things to come:

> Sleep shall neither night nor day
> Hang upon his penthouse lid.

The first section of scene iii is wound up with a charm:

> Thrice to thine and thrice to mine
> And thrice again, to make up nine.

(?) *How does Shakespeare convey a sense of evil and menace through the words of the witches?*

Influence on Macbeth

Power of prophecy

You can see one of the witches' chief dramatic functions in their meeting with Macbeth and Banquo. Notice how Macbeth and Banquo repeat the witches' words, almost as though the witches have some supernatural influence over them. Macbeth says: "So foul and fair a day I have not seen" and Banquo calls the witches "things that do sound so fair." Banquo feels they possess powers of prophecy:

> If you can look into the seeds of time,
> And say which grain will grow and which will not.

The witches foretell Macbeth's future rise to power and Banquo's ability to create kings, but not become one, saying "Thou shalt get kings, though thou be none."

The witches disappear and Macbeth and Banquo are left to discuss the meaning of their words. When they receive the news from Ross and Angus, Macbeth thinks about the prophecies. They seem to have sown the seed of murder in his mind, although the idea of committing murder to fulfil the prophecy begins to disturb him:

> My thought, whose murder yet is but fantastical
> Shakes so my single state of man that function
> Is smother'd in surmise.

He even echoes the witches' form of speech, saying "Time and the hour runs through the roughest day".

Practice Questions

Look at how Macbeth and Banquo react to the prophecies of the witches.

Write a few paragraphs to explain what you think is going through the minds of each of these characters at this stage in the play. Refer to the text to support your ideas.

📺 Persuading Macbeth

◎ *Read Act 1, scene v.*

Finding the meaning

Evil intention

You could say that Lady Macbeth is evil. This kind of interpretation is based on the comments she makes about the letter's contents. Notice how she criticises her husband who is "not without ambition" but doesn't want to get his hands dirty:

> What thou would'st highly
> That would'st thou holily

She regrets that he is a man of integrity who "would'st not play false".

After hearing the messenger's news of Duncan's intention to stay with them, she says she wants to change her personality. She wants to lose her femininity, saying "unsex me here", and be made of nothing but evil:

> And fill me from the crown to the toe top-full
> Of direst cruelty!

She seems determined to be the one to murder Duncan:

> That my keen knife see not the wound it makes.

Does she really relish the prospect of being a killer? Is she steeling herself to do the deed?

(?) *In what ways do the following quotations suggest that Lady Macbeth has a softer side to her nature?*

- *Stop up the access and passage to remorse*

- *Nor heaven peep through the blanket of the dark*

When Macbeth appears, it is Lady Macbeth who appears to be the stronger partner. She is determined that Duncan won't leave their castle alive. She urges Macbeth to disguise his evil intentions.

◎ *Now read Act 1, scene vii.*

Macbeth's doubts

The scene opens with a soliloquy in which Macbeth thinks about the consequence of murder. Killing would be easy if there was to be no judgement:

> That but this blow
> Might be the be-all and end-all here.

There is, however, the judgement to come after death, and the judgement of justice in this life. There is also the problem of Macbeth's troublesome conscience:

Bloody instructions, which, being taught, return
To plague the inventor.

 Macbeth gives his reasons for not murdering the king. Make a list of these reasons. Can you place them in their order of importance?

When Macbeth discusses the proposed murder with his wife, she again appears to be the dominant one of the couple. Macbeth wants to drop the subject:

We will proceed no further in this business.

She tries to shake him out of this attitude:

Was the hope drunk wherein you dress'd yourself?

She calls him a coward. He replies by saying he is no coward:

I dare do all that may become a man.

Lady Macbeth uses the powerful image of dashing out her new born child's brains in order to shame Macbeth. Macbeth wonders if they might fail. Lady Macbeth accepts the possibility of failure but argues that if Macbeth is courageous, they will not fail.

She then outlines her plan. She is the practical one and finally she persuades Macbeth, who says:

I am settled, and bend up
Each corporal agent to this terrible feat.

You can view the relationship between Macbeth and Lady Macbeth in different ways. Do you think she is a dominant character leading her husband down the path of darkness? Or do you see them as a team with different strengths, working together and supporting each other?

Practice Questions

Look at the following two statements:

■ Had it not been for Lady Macbeth's intervention, Macbeth would not have murdered Duncan.

■ Lady Macbeth simply encouraged Macbeth to murder Duncan. He would have done it anyway.

Argue the case for both statements, referring to the text in support of your ideas. Which argument do you feel is the right one?

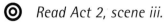
◎ *Read Act 2, scene iii.*

Finding the meaning

In the previous scene Macbeth and Lady Macbeth react in private to the horrors of the murder. Macbeth is distraught, convinced he has murdered "the innocent sleep" and that his hands will never be clean. Scornfully, Lady Macbeth reassures him that "a little water clears us of this deed".

Now we see them having to react in public. They must keep up the appearance of innocence, while at the same time come to terms with their private feelings.

Changes in tone

Dramatic tone

The scene is made more dramatic by the shifts in tone. It opens with dramatic knocking.

Comic tone

The drunken porter's speech is a moment of comedy at a point of high drama. It relieves the tension for a moment, so that what follows will seem more exciting.

❓ *What do you make of the porter's speech? Is it hard to understand? The joke about drink and lechery is obvious enough, but many of the jokes are obscure. Notice, however, the disturbing images, like "Here's a farmer who hanged himself on the expectation of plenty."*

◎ *Jot down some examples of contradictory behaviour given by the porter. Can you find more examples in the rest of the play?*

Light tone

The porter's drunken behaviour makes Macduff and Lennox think that there has been a celebration. This lightens the tone, since the last thing the visitors would expect is that murder had been committed. When Macbeth appears he sustains this mood with idle banter:

| *Macduff:* | I know this is a joyful trouble to you. |
| *Macbeth:* | The labour we delight in physics pain. |

Darker tone

The mood darkens with Lennox's description of the night. Nature seemed to have been at war with the Earth:

Some say the earth
Was fevorous and did shake.

The tension reaches a new climax with Macduff's dramatic entrance:

O horror, horror, horror!

Without meaning to, he reminds Macbeth of one of his reasons for not wishing to kill Duncan, i.e. Duncan's divine right to be king:

Most sacriligeous murder hath broke ope
The Lord's anointed temple.

Yet Macbeth remains calm, asking innocent questions. Macduff heightens the dramatic tension by demanding an alarm bell should be rung.

On her entry Lady Macbeth plays the innocent. Macduff is convinced by her act and tries to protect her from news of the murder:

'Tis not for you to hear what I can speak!

When the news does break, Lady Macbeth's only concern is that it should have been committed in her house. Macbeth, however, is deeply disturbed. He wishes he had died before the murder. The murder has apparently changed the way he thinks about life, as he says: "There's nothing serious in mortality." To Donalbain's innocent question, "What's amiss?" Macbeth replies in strong terms. After Lennox's vivid description of the dead grooms, Macbeth admits to having killed them.

Use of language

Think about the speech beginning: "Who can be wise, amazed, temperate and furious ...". What does the language tell you about Macbeth's state of mind? Why do you think he describes the murder scene in such vivid detail? Is it because his horror at Duncan's appearance, he hopes, will prove his innocence, or has Macbeth been fascinated by what he has done? He says:

His silver skin laced with his golden blood.

The richness of the language could indicate a morbid fascination.

It's difficult to decide if Banquo knows who killed Duncan. His words are ambiguous. He speaks of "fears and scruples", almost as if he fears he knows who did the deed, but he has scruples in view of his relationship with Macbeth. Remember, of course, that both Banquo and Macbeth heard the witches' prophecies. Banquo certainly calls the murder "treasonous malice".

! REMEMBER
Examiners like you to show that you are aware of different interpretations of the characters' words and actions.

17

Macbeth

(?) *Lady Macbeth faints. Do you think this is a genuine reaction or is it an attempt to divert people's attention? After her dramatic faint, Malcolm and Donalbain quietly contemplate their position. Do they decide to flee Scotland or Macbeth? What do you think?*

Practice Questions

1 How do Macbeth and Lady Macbeth react to the announcement of the murder of Duncan?

2 Do you consider their reactions to be genuine, an attempt to fool the others, or a mixture of both? Give reasons for your answer.

ⓣⓥ The banquet

◎ *Read Act 3, scene iv.*

In this scene Macbeth is forced to face up to the reality of the evil he has done. First he is responsible for the death of Duncan, king by divine authority. Now he has hired murderers to dispatch Banquo and his son Fleance, so that the witches' prophecy might be fulfilled.

Finding the meaning

The scene opens like any normal dinner party. Macbeth bids everyone a "hearty welcome" and says he will "play the humble host". At the murderers' news that Fleance has "'scaped" Macbeth hints that his mind is becoming unhinged:

> Then comes my fit again.

◎ *Look closely at Macbeth's reaction to the news that Fleance has escaped. He feels: "cabin'd, cribbed, confined". What do these words suggest? What ideas are revealed through the images of the serpent and the worm?*

Macbeth tries to rid his mind of doubts and turns his attention to his guests:

> Now good digestion wait on appetite,
> And health on both!

He even wishes that Banquo were at the feast. Almost as if prompted by this, Banquo's ghost takes his place at the table. Shocked, Macbeth at first puts the blame on his guests, asking "Which of you have done this?"

He addresses the ghost directly. Lady Macbeth, as she had done in the scene following Duncan's murder, tries to divert criticism:

> The fit is momentary ... feed and regard him not.

Macbeth returns to his predicament which haunts him throughout the play. While he is brave on the battlefield, he finds murder unnatural:

> Ay, and a bold one, that dare look on that
> Which might appal the devil.

Lady Macbeth reminds him of his vision of a dagger that led him towards Duncan's bed chamber. Macbeth insists there is a ghost. The imagery indicates Macbeth's unhinged mind:

> Our monuments
> Shall be the maws of our kites.

Killing and burying his victims will not solve his problems. He imagines the graves spewing the bodies back into the world. Macbeth feels the dead will return to get their revenge. You can feel the horror in his words:

The time has been
That, when the brains were out, the man would die,
And there an end; but now they rise again.

Macbeth is persuaded to rejoin the guests. Notice how Macbeth wavers between normality and insanity in this scene. At one moment he plays the host as if nothing had happened. The next he is appalled by the apparition.

On the ghost's next appearance, Macbeth returns to his obsessive fear, saying that he can face any normal danger bravely ("my firm nerves shall never tremble"). To Macbeth the ghost is so palpably present he believes his wife must see it too. It is at this point that Lady Macbeth bids their guests leave immediately, putting aside formalities:

Stand not upon the order of your going.

 Imagine you were a guest at the banquet. Write down what you saw and heard and your thoughts about these strange events.

The break-up of the party is a kind of visual image of Macbeth's mental breakdown. On the guests' departure, he muses on his private fears:

It will have blood; they say blood will have blood.

He is beginning to believe in the supernatural world of the witches:

Stones have been known to move and trees speak.

In fact, he is determined to visit the witches again to confirm his worst fears. There can be no going back on his murderous intentions:

I am in blood
Stepp'd in so far that, should I wade no more
Returning were as tedious as go o'er.

Banquo's apparition has convinced him. He is now determined on his evil course, though he sees it as an inevitable and tedious one. Lady Macbeth, however, thinks there is hope, if only he could sleep. She says:

You lack the season of all natures, sleep.

Macbeth disagrees. His way ahead is more killing. It is as if he is saying they have only just begun:

We are yet but young in deed.

Is it this – the realisation that there is more horror to come – which finally causes Lady Macbeth's insanity?

Practice Questions

The ghost of Banquo reflects Macbeth's troubled state of mind. It is also a reminder of the forces of darkness. When they put on the play, some directors choose not to physically represent the ghost, others do so.

How do you think the ghost should be portrayed? Explain, giving your reasons.

The end of Lady Macbeth

◎ *Read Act 5, scene i.*

Finding the meaning

The audience enters the nightmare world of Lady Macbeth's mind. Shakespeare uses the dialogue between the Doctor and a Waiting-Gentlewoman to prepare for her entry. When the audience sees Lady Macbeth sleep walking, it is reminded of Macbeth's prophetic words "Macbeth does murder sleep".

Lady Macbeth speaks disjointedly. In her apparent rambling, notice how her mind relives the key moments in her life.

◎ *Look at Lady Macbeth's speeches in this scene. Make a list of quotations and events from earlier scenes in the play to which she is referring.*

Her concerns reveal her state of mind now, but they also recall her former self. For example, "Yet who would have thought the old man to have had so much blood in him" is a reference to their blood-stained hands after the murder of Duncan. In the same way, the never-ending washing of her hands and her complaint: "What, will these hands ne'er be clean?" is an ironic reference to the advice she gave to her husband in Act 2, scene ii:

A little water will clear us of this deed.

Notice that in the heat of the moment she felt their guilt would be quickly and easily washed away. Now, in her mind she realises that she will never be able to get rid of her guilt.

She also carries the burden of her husband's fear. She is obsessed by the terror her husband felt in the banquet scene. Then he spoke of his fear that the dead would rise and "push us from our stools". She says about his dilemma:

I tell you yet again, Banquo's buried; he cannot come out on's grave.

Her madness is conveyed in several ways. You'll have already noted that her thoughts appear to be spoken at random, but there is a kind of insane logic in them. She speaks in prose. She has rejected the fine verse of a queen's speech. All she has left is her basic humanity. She appears obsessed with key symbols of the play: blood, standing for guilt; and water, representing longed-for forgiveness. Finally, she invites pity for her condition by referring to her hand as "little".

Interpretation

Because the words are simple and the expression disjointed, you can interpret them in a variety of ways.

◎ *Read Lady Macbeth's speeches from this scene aloud. Decide how much feeling to put into them and, more importantly, how much to leave out. Test your interpretation against what you have learned about the character of Lady Macbeth earlier in the play.*

Changes in mood

◎ *Read Act 5, scene iii, after the entrance of Seyton. Also read Act 5, scene v, up to the point where a messenger enters.*

When the Doctor speaks of Lady Macbeth's "thick coming fancies", Macbeth orders him to cure her. He asks:

> Can'st thou not minister to a mind diseased,
> Pluck from the memory a rooted sorrow?

He is speaking of his wife's predicament. But is it a cry from his own heart? He, too, may be longing for "some sweet, oblivious antidote". Nevertheless he soon dismisses that mood and dispatches physic "to the dogs".

Immediately he becomes involved in the task of defending Dunsinane Castle. He says he has "almost forgot the taste of fears".

> Direness, familiar to my slaughterous thoughts,
> Cannot once start me.

When Seyton announces the death of the Queen, though, Macbeth's mood changes. He becomes fatalistic and philosophical about the meaning of existence. Life, he says, is very brief:

> Out, out, brief candle!

A person is as insignificant as a poor actor. Personal fame is soon forgotten:

> ... a poor player
> That struts and frets his hour upon the stage
> And then is heard no more.

Life itself is meaningless, "signifying nothing".

All Macbeth has left to believe in is the witches prophecies that he will not be defeated until "Birnam Forest come to Dunsinane" and that he cannot be killed by anyone who is "not born of woman". His wife has been broken by the tragic events of their lives. He will survive by clinging to the belief in prophecies which, finally, prove to be false.

Practice Questions

1 In what ways are Macbeth and Lady Macbeth shown to suffer for the crimes they have committed?

2 For whom do you feel the most sympathy? Explain your choice.

⊙ Finding the meaning

Over the years, the **critics** have argued about what the poem "The Tyger" means. There are many different **interpretations**, or ideas about the meaning. When you answer exam questions it's important to have your own ideas too.

To impress the examiner, you must show that you've thought about the poem yourself. If you haven't become involved in it – it will show in your answer.

To find the meaning:

- **read the poem** through carefully several times
- **brainstorm** it, jotting down your ideas about what you think it means
- select the **key ideas**
- find **evidence** in the poem to support these ideas
- write down **new ideas** that occur to you

Read it through

When you come to a poem for the first time, read it through several times. Always try to read it through at least once.

Brainstorm it

Here are some of the ideas that the critics have had about "The Tyger", presented as a brainstorm:

 REMEMBER It usually helps to brainstorm a poem and look for all possible meanings.

religious, like a
prayer, a hymn,
a spell

mysterious,
has a beat

maybe "He" is God

is it a real tiger?

tiger is a
metaphor for
the whole of
nature

magnificent, terrible
– is the tiger bad?

The Tyger

contrast with a lamb

poem has force

creator took a
chance
when he made
the tiger

tiger is a jungle cat –
muscle in the heart

what was he releasing?

clear picture of jungle,
hunting and prey

Select key ideas

Now sort out those ideas that fit your own thoughts about the poem.

 Underline the points in the brainstorm list that best match your ideas about "The Tyger".
Add any other ideas that you have about the poem.

Find the evidence

Read the poem again and look for words, phrases or lines that reflect or support the points you have underlined. For example, you might agree that Blake shows the tiger as being "magnificent and terrible". A phrase that reflects this is "fearful symmetry".

 Underline the words and phrases you have chosen.

New ideas

Now look at the poem and see what's left. You might find lines such as:

Did he who made the Lamb make thee?

This could lead you to add ideas about a creation to the brainstorm. This way of working is vitally important.

Right or wrong?

Many people say that a poem can mean anything, because there is no right or wrong answer. There is a right answer – but not one that the examiner is keeping up his or her sleeve. The right answer lies in the ideas you have and the evidence you find for these in the poem. Examiners will recognise your ability to develop ideas and to support them with reference to the poem.

> **! REMEMBER** Always work on the poem itself. Underline key words and phrases and write brief comments by the side.

> **! REMEMBER** Always look for evidence in the text of the poem to support your ideas.

Blake

23

Practice Questions

1 For each of the following ideas write down a quotation from "The Tyger" to support it:

- the poem presents a picture of a real tiger
- the tiger is evil
- the poem is mysterious
- the poem has great force
- the poem's images are vivid
- the poem asks questions about the creator

- the poem has a tremendous beat
- the creator took a chance with his creation
- the poem is really about the nature of human beings
- the poem reflects the industrial revolution

2 Select another of Blake's poems. Brainstorm it. Match your ideas with evidence from the poem.

Understanding the writer

In order to understand his poetry, it helps to know some key facts about Blake's childhood:

- he was born into a rebellious family
- his parents did not accept the practices of the Church of England
- he was a solitary child who read the Bible
- he refused to go to school
- he hated authority
- he saw visions of God and angels
- he became aware of **social injustice**

Expressing his views

Blake's poems reflect both his own character and his concerns about what was happening around him.

◎ *Write down the following key subject headings. Under each heading name one of Blake's poems in which you think he writes about the subject. A poem may appear under more than one heading.*

SOCIAL INJUSTICE   RELIGION   HUMAN NATURE   REBELLION

Blake was a **revolutionary**, but he was not the sort to go on protest marches. He expressed his revolutionary ideas in his own way through his poetry.

Anger

In "London" Blake writes about the city he knew so well. He is angry about what he sees: the suffering of the infants, the chimney sweeps, the soldiers and the young prostitutes.

Hatred

Behind the signs of poverty and despair he sees something else which is very important to him.

London is "charter'd", ie. the streets have become "official". The River Thames, instead of being a part of nature, has become a part of the **establishment** Blake so despised.

He has found a way to express his hatred of everything official (school, church, state) in the way that the streets and the river have become almost a part of government policy.

24

> **REMEMBER**
> Try to do some background reading. The examiner will reward the results of your research.

> **REMEMBER**
> Be aware of how a poet's writing has been influenced by events in his or her life.

Horror

Look at the second stanza. Blake is appalled by the cries of suffering he hears on the streets of London. But who, according to Blake, is the cause of this suffering? Not the government. Blake thinks our chains ("manacles") are produced by our own minds. In a sense, he is saying that we are all responsible for what is happening around us.

Levels of expression

Blake is a revolutionary writer who expresses his horror at different levels:

■ he sees the people suffering on the streets of London

■ he looks beneath the surface to find the real causes of social injustice

■ he looks into our minds and asks us if we should change our attitudes

◎ *Make a list of the things that disturb Blake as he walks London's streets.*
In what ways are these images relevant to the present day?

Life's struggle

◎ *Re-read "Infant Sorrow".*

In this poem, Blake writes:

　　　　I thought best
　To sulk upon my mother's breast.

Here is an example of rebellion – the young child refusing to co-operate. Blake sees our life as a struggle. Mother "groaned", father "wept". The child is "struggling in my father's arms." In the last line of the poem the child decides to wait for the next round of the struggle. Until then he will sulk.

⁇ *What have you learnt about Blake's views on life from reading "London" and "Infant Sorrow"?*

REMEMBER Look for different levels of meaning in a poem. You can find clues in the way a poet uses words that surprise or puzzle the reader.

25

REMEMBER The examiner will reward candidates who are aware of ideas that link poems together.

Blake

Practice Questions

Look at the poem "Infant Sorrow".

1 Why do you think Blake presents childhood in this way?

2 Is it just his own personal view of things? (Remember that the young Blake was a solitary, rebellious child.)

3 Is this a realistic portrayal of infancy?

4 Why do you think the poet has painted the first stages of life in this way?

ⓣ Use of language

Blake often uses simple language – short words and words that are heard in everyday speech. But in Blake's hands they are rarely as simple and straightforward as they might appear. One reason is that he often uses a word as a **symbol**.

What is a symbol?

A symbol is a word that describes something and what it represents. For example, the words "traffic lights" describe an object that tells traffic when to stop and go. The words also represent authority, so "traffic lights" are a symbol of authority.

Finding symbols

◎　*Re-read "The Sick Rose".*

Blake writes about a rose attacked by a worm, which destroys it. He introduces other elements, which affect how we view the rose:

- the worm is invisible
- there is a howling storm
- the rose is a bed, in which there is crimson joy

⁇　*Can you begin to see the rose as more than just a flower – as a symbol of something?*

Symbol of love

The rose could be a symbol of love. Here, the love is "dark" and "secret".

◎　*Does this affect how we should see the rose? Is this why the worm can destroy the life of the rose? Write down what you think.*

Finding more meaning

The more you read this poem, the more meanings and ideas you'll see.

- Is the worm the serpent in the Garden of Eden?
- Is the rose "crimson" because it is blushing, ashamed of this secret affair?
- Why is the rose "sick"? Is it because of the worm, or was the rose ill before the worm finds it out?

REMEMBER Always be alert to the different things with which a word can be associated. Try checking out a word's associations in a thesaurus.

REMEMBER Always be on the look-out for different meanings and other possible interpretations.

Several meanings

One symbol can have several different meanings with different effects. When you are writing exam answers, don't give a symbol one meaning only. For instance, don't write:

The rose is a flower set in The Garden of Eden. "Crimson" means the guilt Adam and Eve felt when they realised they were naked. The worm is the serpent which comes to tempt Eve.

Try to be open and suggest different ideas. You might write:

The rose seems to be about human love. The love seems to be guilty as though the lovers are embarrassed ("crimson joy"). Blake is perhaps referring to the Garden of Eden ("the invisible worm"), and the way Adam and Eve felt.

! REMEMBER Don't be too precise in saying that one word definitely means one thing only.

Personal symbols

Blake had his own individual symbols. For him, some words represented definite ideas or feelings.

For example, the words *field, hills, valleys, meadows, plains, green* – all found in *Songs of Innocence* – represented for Blake uninhibited joy.

On the other hand, a rose meant experienced love, guilt and shame.

Such words formed part of his vision and meant he could express his ideas in a very personal way.

? *To understand symbols further, think about what the following flowers mean to you:*
- *a rose*
- *a poppy*
- *a thistle*
- *a snowdrop*

Colours can also have symbolic meaning. What do you associate the following colours with: black, white, red, grey?

Blake

Practice Questions

Re-read "The Sick Rose" and "The Poison Tree."

What do you think each of the following words might represent in these poems?

rose worm storm bed tree apple garden night

Write a few sentences on each word, describing what you think they could represent. Remember to check your ideas against the evidence contained in the poems.

The importance of sound

When you answer exam questions on poetry, you'll be expected to recognise the **rhymes** and **rhythms** of the verse. Examiners will expect you to be able to show how they make a poem more effective. It's essential that you get used to reading poetry aloud. This will help you become more sensitive to rhyme and rhythm.

Poets use rhyme and rhythm for a specific purpose – to emphasise and reflect on what they are trying to say. Blake was no exception.

Rhyme and rhythm

! REMEMBER
Feel the rhythm of a poem by reading it aloud.

Questions

◎ *Re-read "The Lamb".*

The use of questions and answers in this poem help to give the verse a rhythm. Notice how the first stanza is full of questions. Blake gives the answers to the questions in the second stanza.

Rhyming couplets

Blake uses rhyming couplets to tie the two stanzas of the poem closer together. He has used the word "thee" to emphasise the questions and underline the answers.

! REMEMBER
Find the basic pattern but notice the exceptions – these are important.

Same sounds

The overall "ee" sound runs like a theme through the poem. Notice how Blake uses **assonance** (similar sounds) at the beginnings as well at the ends of lines:

- Gave th<u>ee</u> life
- By the str<u>ea</u>m
- Gave th<u>ee</u> clothing
- Gave th<u>ee</u> such
- H<u>e</u> is m<u>ee</u>k
- W<u>e</u> are called

The "ee" sound echoes throughout the poem, like the sound of a bleating lamb. It gives a tender feel to the language to reflect the lamb's innocence.

Repetitive words

Blake also uses a trick called **foregrounding**. The technique consists of starting statements with the same words:

Little Lamb, I'll tell thee
Little Lamb, I'll tell thee.

The words may not always be exactly the same, but the sentence construction is.

 Can you find other examples of foregrounding in the poem?

The effect of this repetition is to highlight key ideas and impress them on the reader's mind. Blake prevents this from becoming boring by introducing subtle variations into the word patterns:

"He is called"/"We are called"

Some poems contain **refrains**:

Little Lamb, God bless thee!
Little Lamb, God bless thee.

REMEMBER
Look for repetition of words and ideas. Why did the poet write like this?

The chiming effects of the rhymes and assonance help to preserve the feeling of innocence. Notice how Blake repeats the word "lamb" to express different ideas about the nature of the Lamb. In one line Christ is the Lamb of God. In another a child takes on the Lamb's nature and therefore that of Christ himself.

Re-read "A Poison Tree".

Here Blake uses many of the devices already considered, such as rhyming couplets and foregrounding. He makes effective use of repetitive sounds. The insistent "and" gives the poem a sense of urgency. The story is told chiefly in monosyllables:

And he knew that it was mine
And into my garden stole

until the climax of the poem where Blake slows the pace with the two words "outstretched beneath".

Blake

Practice Questions

1 Find and write down one example of each of the following from "A Poison Tree":

■ rhyming couplets
■ foregrounding
■ repetition

2 Show how rhyme and rhythm are important features in "The Lamb" and "A Poison Tree". Support the points you make with reference to the text.

⊙ The importance of tone

If you can discuss a poem's **tone**, you will really impress the examiner. It will prove that you can read a poem with sensitivity and understand not just what a poet has to say, but *the way* in which he or she says it.

Understanding tone

❗ R E M E M B E R
Read poems aloud and feel the tone that the poet is using. Listen to recordings of the poems.

The best way to understand tone is to read aloud a poem you are studying. It's useful to tape your readings and listen to them over and over so that you really get to know them.

Different tones

 Read aloud "The Tyger" and "The Lamb". Can you feel the difference between the urgent, passionate tone of "The Tyger" and the childlike tone of "The Lamb"?

Similar tones

The two poems appear quite separate in their tone. But there are, in fact, similarities. In both Blake adopts a questioning tone, as though he is marvelling at these different aspects of creation. There is also a feeling of wonder common to both.

◉ *Find two examples of questions from each poem. Consider different ways of how they could be read aloud.*

Shifts in tone

❗ R E M E M B E R
Always be ready for the shifts in tone which indicate a change of mood. You will receive extra credit if you can recognise them.

Reading a poem can be like listening to a friend speaking to you. Your friend might be angry or sad or happy and their tone of voice would reflect their feelings. Then their mood might change. Just as your friend's voice can change during conversation, the tone of a poem can alter.

Re-read "A Poison Tree." Notice how the tone of the first stanza is one of personal anger. Blake's angry feelings are directed at friend and foe. The heavy rhythm serves to emphasise the mood: "I told it not, my wrath did grow."

As the poet describes how his "wrath did grow", the pace picks up. As the story unfolds you feel the writer's pleasure in telling the story of his growing wrath. You feel his sense of wrong when his foe stole into his garden. Finally the pace slows on "outstretched beneath". This allows the poet time to enjoy his moment of triumph.

Conversational tone

Now read aloud "Infant Joy" (*Innocence*). This poem takes the form of a conversation between a mother and her baby. You will notice the sweet, innocent tone, particularly in the second stanza where the mother is expressing her joy. On the surface it seems wholly natural that the mother should delight in her child:

> Thou dost smile
> I sing the while.

Notice the way the infant speaks in the poem. How matter-of-fact:

> I have no name:
> I am but two days old.

It is the child who tells the mother her name:

> I happy am
> Joy is my name.

Notice also the use of exclamations and the repetition of particular words and phrases.

- ◎ *Read the poem with a friend as a conversation between the infant and the mother. Note the ways in which the words are spoken.*

- ⟨?⟩ *The shifts in tone between mother and child are quite puzzling. Why do you think the infant speaks in such a matter-of-fact tone, while the mother responds in the tone you would expect in such a situation?*

> **R E M E M B E R**
> Try to feel the subtle changes in a poem's overall tone.

Blake

Practice Questions

Choose two of the following poems:

- "The Tyger"
- "The Lamb"
- "A Poison Tree"
- "Infant Joy"

1 Write about the tone of each poem, noting any changes or shifts.

2 Explain how Blake manages to convey the tones you have identified.
You should consider each of the following:

- rhythm
- repetition
- use of language

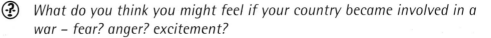

"Peace" by Rupert Brooke

The poets who wrote at the time of the First World War were affected by it in different ways. In the beginning, before they experienced the horrors of trench warfare, some poets wrote about the wonderful opportunities war offered the young men of Britain.

(?) *What do you think you might feel if your country became involved in a war – fear? anger? excitement?*

◎ *Read "Peace" by Rupert Brooke.*

Meaning

As you can see, the poem's title is ironic: it is not about peace. Brooke welcomes the chance to go to war and thanks God for it. He believes that war has given young people something to do:

> and wakened us from sleeping

He thinks that England has become "a world grown old and cold and weary" and that people were not achieving the most they could. They were "half-men". War would do England good.

◎ *List words and phrases that show how Brooke feels about England. Explain what difference he thinks war will make.*

Language

Brooke conveys his attitude to war not only by what he says, but by:

- the words he uses

- the ways he puts words together

He sees war as a God-given opportunity. The first four lines sound triumphant, celebrating this opportunity. The young have been "wakened". Up till now their lives have been spent simply "sleeping". Brooke sees the chance to fight as a chance for English men to cleanse themselves. War will be a kind of purification:

> To turn, as swimmers into cleanness leaping

The word "leaping" suggests that men will go to war with energy and enthusiasm. The line also marks a change in the poem as the focus shifts to peacetime Britain. All the images now are negative ones:

- a world grown old
- sick hearts
- half-men
- dirty songs and dreary

Honour, he says, cannot move these men. He even shows love as a small and empty experience.

◎ *Look at the list you have already made and the phrases listed on the previous page.*
Explain how they present a depressed picture of peacetime Britain.
Now compare them to these phrases from the first five lines of the poem:

- caught our youth
- clear eye
- wakened us from sleeping
- sharpened power
- hand made sure
- into cleanness leaping

Tone

The poem sounds like a kind of prayer. It begins with words of praise to the Lord:

> Now God be thanked Who has
> matched us with His hour

The word "and" is repeated seven times in the poem. This creates a sense of continuity and lets the poet link each idea closely to the one before and the one after it.

The rhymes also tie the ideas together. Sometimes the effect is one of contrast:

"wakened us from sleeping" and "into cleanness leaping".

At other times Brooke uses the rhyme to stress the decay in society:

"cold and weary" and "dirty songs and dreary".

The poet pairs words to reinforce the ideas:

"a world grown old" is also "cold and weary";

the "hand made sure" is accompanied by a "clear eye".

Brooke is perhaps so enthusiastic in his celebration of war because he wants to encourage his readers to volunteer for service. The poem captures the national mood of optimism which existed when it was written. Many people believed that war would be a good thing and, after all, it would be over in six weeks and the men would be home by Christmas.

! R E M E M B E R
Always be aware of how the War Poets use religious ideas and words.

World War I Poetry

Practice Questions

Show how Brooke organises his ideas and uses language to persuade his reader that the announcement of war is a thing to be celebrated.

⊙ "The Soldier" by Rupert Brooke

◎ *Read "The Soldier" by Rupert Brooke*

Meaning

This poem was written as Brooke prepared to leave to fight in Turkey. In it he foresees his death in a foreign country. He believes that when he dies and his body turns to dust, it will be a better, "richer" dust than the earth in which it will be buried. The reason is that his dust will have been made by all the good things which are to be found in England:

> A body of England's breathing English air,
> Washed by the rivers, blest by suns of home.

For him, this is not a matter for sadness. In death, his body will give back those values learned in England, the values which he feels are so important:

> Laughter learned of friends; and gentleness,
> In hearts at peace, under an English heaven.

Brooke uses the word "England" repeatedly throughout the poem. It represents not only a country, or a place, but a set of values. We all come from dust, the poet is saying, but he has the advantage of being shaped by English dust.

⁇ *How does Brooke present England as a kind of paradise?*
Compare this view of England with the view he presented in "Peace".

Form

❗ REMEMBER Do not explain in the examination what a sonnet is. But do show the examiner that you understand how a poet uses the sonnet.

Brooke has chosen to write his poem as a sonnet, a form commonly used by poets when they want to express personal feelings. This sonnet is divided into two stanzas. The first contains eight lines (an octet) and the second contains six lines (a sestet). Each has its own rhyme scheme. In the first stanza it is AB AB CD CD. The second is EFG EFG. The rhyme schemes separate the stanzas, but they also bind the ideas together in each stanza.

First stanza

The first stanza is concerned with the possibility that the poet may be killed abroad and his body buried in a foreign country.

Second stanza

The subject of the poem turns on the word "and" at the beginning of the second stanza. Here Brooke considers what his death can give back to England or to the next generation.

Here are some possible reasons why Brooke chose the sonnet form:

■ it is a very classical and regular form like the verse that might be found on a gravestone

■ it is a good way of expressing personal ideas

■ the separate stanzas help the poet to deal with related ideas

◎ *Explain how Brooke uses the two stanza form of the sonnet to look at separate, though related, ideas.*

Tone

The overall tone of "The Soldier" is one of personal reflection. A religious feel is given by the rather formal movement of the verse. Brooke uses phrases connected with religious ceremony:

■ think only this

■ that is forever

■ there shall be

The balanced phrases within the line make it seem formal:

"A body of England's" is balanced by "breathing English air".

"Washed by the rivers" has its counterpart "blest by suns of home".

The poet gives to lines an air of formality by first stating an idea and then developing it:

"A dust whom England bore" goes on to be "shaped, made aware".

There is a sense of lightness and calm created through the focus on happy memories:

"Her sights and sounds","Dreams happy as her day", "And, laughter, learnt of friends"

These features combine to give the feeling of a man contemplating his coming death. There is sadness since his body will be turned to dust, but also a quiet feeling of optimism, that his death will have some purpose. The values he has learnt will be given back. He will not have died in vain.

World War I Poetry

Practice Questions

1 Explain the viewpoint presented by Brooke in this poem. What are your thoughts and feelings about this?

2 What effect do you think it would have on someone whose loved one was at war?

⊚ "Attack" by Siegfried Sassoon

Poets who fought at the front were faced with the harsh realities of war. Their writing reflected their experiences. The patriotic feelings of Brooke's poetry were soon replaced by quite different emotions brought out by the mud and slaughter of the trenches.

◎ *Read "Attack" by Siegfried Sassoon.*

Meaning

There is a clear difference between Sassoon's experience and that of Brooke. The difference is reflected in what he writes about. Sassoon wanted people to know what was going on. In "Attack", he writes about an actual dawn raid. He describes the men going over the top into battle.

His poem is concerned with the pointlessness of war. He writes, not of heroism or idealism, but of the reality of trench warfare:

> tanks creep and topple forward to the wire

(?) *What do you think the people at home would have learnt about trench warfare from reading this poem?*

He writes from actual experience. He describes precisely the way tanks moved on the battlefield. The gunfire is real:

> The barrage roars and lifts

He captures the moment of men floundering in mud. He states what happens, as a war reporter might:

> They leave their trenches, going over the top

He ends with a desperate plea for this kind of slaughter to stop.

(?) Language

❗ **REMEMBER** Concentrate in your answers on HOW the poet presents his experience of war.

The poem is made up of three long sentences broken up by the short statement "The barrage roars and lifts". It is as though Sassoon is piling one detail on top of the other, reflecting the grim inevitability of the whole process. The abrupt exclamation at the end is a sign of desperation and an attempt to involve the reader in that feeling.

There are strong images throughout the poem. The "glow'ring sun" is portrayed as:

> Smouldering through spouts of drifting smoke that shroud
> The menacing scarred slope

◎ *Think about the effects of the words "glow'ring", "smouldering", "drifting", "shroud", "menacing", and "scarred" as they appear in this image. How do they create a sense of danger and death? Write down your ideas.*

Personification

In the above example the slope is described as "menacing". It is given a human characteristic to suggest it is both threatening and dangerous. This form of imagery is known as personification – the object becomes like a person. Sassoon uses personification a lot in this poem.

 Think about these images:

- *time ticks blank and busy on their wrists*
- *hope, with furtive eyes and grappling fists, flounders in mud*

Explain how Sassoon has personified time and hope. Do you think these images are effective?

Tone

There is a sense of distancing in this poem. The whole scene is shrouded in mist and the soldiers are not shown as individuals, but as an indistinct group with their faces hidden:

Lines of grey, muttering faces, masked with fear

Although Sassoon describes in detail what is happening, there is a sense of unreality to the scene – almost like a dream or nightmare.

The poem moves relentlessly on almost as if the writer is in a trance. The sun rises and the tanks move forward as the men leave their trenches. As they flounder in the mud, the poet can bear it no longer and he cries out:

Jesus, make it stop!

This is the cry of a real man in a real situation. The colloquial outburst breaking into the trance-like atmosphere pulls the reader back to reality. It is as if the poet is waking from a nightmare. He hopes his cry will be heard back home.

World War I Poetry

Practice Questions

Compare the poems "Attack" and "The Soldier".

1 What is the same or different about their subject matter?

2 In what ways do Brooke and Sassoon use language effectively to convey their ideas to the reader?

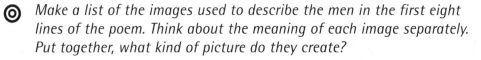 "Dulce et Decorum Est" by Wilfred Owen

Like Sassoon, Owen was appalled by what was going on in the war. He intensified the attack on those responsible for the fighting and tried to undermine the belief that war was glorious.

◎ *Read "Dulce et Decorum Est" by Wilfred Owen.*

Meaning

> **REMEMBER** Always be aware of the mixture of reality and unreality in the work of the War Poets.

As in "Attack", Owen mixes reality and unreality to get his message across. But in Owen's poetry the sense of reality is more vivid. He describes a scene of war, made more vivid by his own involvement:

> we cursed through sludge

He draws the reader into the poem by comparing his situation to a more familiar one, "like old beggars under sacks". He takes the reader along with them on their march, saying: "Men marched asleep" and "All went lame; all blind." He recreates the start of a gas attack:

> Gas! GAS! Quick boys!

He shows that the man has to shout "Gas" louder a second time, because the men are too tired to hear.

Next there is a bitter description of the man who doesn't put on his gas mask in time. The image of the man helplessly "drowning" in the gas is one that haunts his sleep and one which he feels he has to share with his reader:

> If you could hear...

Owen's anger at this waste of life is shown in his description of the man's suffering, "obscene as cancer".

◎ *Imagine you're a soldier in Owen's regiment who witnessed this scene. Describe what you experienced and saw. Try to avoid using the language of the poem.*

Language

The poem falls into four stages:

- the men marching
- the gas attack where the man fails to put on his gas mask
- the events following this
- the appeal to the reader

◎ *Make a list of the images used to describe the men in the first eight lines of the poem. Think about the meaning of each image separately. Put together, what kind of picture do they create?*

Now look at lines 9–16. When the attack comes, the fumbling for a gas mask is described as "ecstasy" – the most heightened of sensations. The soldier who doesn't fit his in time is like "a man in fire or lime". The poem becomes dream-like as Owen sees him dimly through his own mask. The scene is like being "under a green sea" and the man is "drowning".

In the final stanza, the ugly and bitter images create a sense of wickedness and evil. The man is flung into the wagon, his eyes "writhing" and his face a "devil's sick of sin". The adjectives "froth-corrupted", "obscene", "bitter", "vile" and "incurable" follow one after another, leaving the reader in no doubt of the horror of the scene.

Suddenly the horror stops. The reader is addressed as "My friend" and finally Owen speaks out about the "old lie" which England has been suffering from. He expresses it in Latin:

Dulce et decorum est
Pro patria mori

This means "it is sweet and noble to die for one's country". Would the people who preach about war say the same thing if they had seen what Owen had seen?

Latin, a dead language, was an important subject in the public school education of Owen's day. The poet uses it to show how out of touch, how dead, the old system of education was, particularly when it spread the lie that it was sweet and noble to die for one's native country.

Tone

The tone is bitter and sarcastic. The poet's anger is felt in the cutting alliteration: "Bent double like old beggars".

The harsh consonants convey his feelings:

Come gargling from froth-corrupted lungs

Mixed in with the harsh reality are the dream-like passages where Owen softens the tone:

Dim through the misty panes and thick green light

Here, the gentle consonants and softer sounds of the words give a muffled effect. This shifting from the harsh reality of battle to a trance-like state, and back again, is very effective. Owen is suggesting the state of mind of the exhausted troops. They are engaged in a real fight, but it all seems unreal.

Practice Questions

1 How does Owen try to convince the reader that war is evil? You should consider: patterns, ideas, language, tone.

2 After reading "Dulce Et Decorum Est", has Owen convinced you that war is evil? If so, explain how he has. If not, describe the ways in which he has failed to convince you.

3 How successful do you think the poem is?

"Strange Meeting" by Wilfred Owen

Unlike "Dulce Et Decorum Est", where Owen starts in the middle of the fighting, here he begins by escaping from the battlefield.

Meaning

Owen imagines that one of the tunnels, in which soldiers took cover from shellfire, led deeper to where a group of sleeping men was to be found. He can't decide whether they are asleep or dead.

When he prods one of the figures, the man jumps up and Owen realises from his gestures that they are both in hell. The poet is surprised that no blood seeped down from the trenches or there was no sound of gunfire as there would have been in a frontline tunnel.

This "strange friend" reveals what the war has meant for him – wasted years, the loss of true beauty, and, much worse, the truth which has been suppressed:

> The pity of war, the pity war distilled

The friend goes on to say that future generations will have to put up with what they have ruined. He would like to bring back lost innocence:

> I would go up and wash them from sweet wells

He would have made every effort:

> I would have poured my spirit without stint

He wanted to save the world, but not through war, which he calls a "cess" (an open sewer). He then confesses that he is the enemy the poet killed. He recognises Owen because he is wearing the same expression that he wore when he killed him:

> for so you frowned
> Yesterday through me as you jabbed and killed.

He concludes by suggesting that they should "sleep now".

◉ *Read through the poem carefully – preferably aloud – making sure you understand its meaning.*

Language

Owen creates a vision of hell, but it is a hell which grows out of the battlefield, the soldier's own hell: "dull tunnel", "guns thumped or down the flues made moan".

The well-known places and events of war are exaggerated in the poem. The tunnels have been "scooped through granites". The war is described as a struggle between the gods ("Titanic wars"). The poem refers to more ancient wars, "when much blood had clogged their chariot wheels", as though the Great War encompasses all wars.

In his regret for his lost youth the strange friend speaks of lost ideals of hope and beauty. He talks of lost opportunities for laughter:

For by my glee might many men have laughed.

Tone

The overall tone is one of regret. Owen is sickened by the waste and loss, but he does not sound angry. Everything happens in a dream-like atmosphere. The whole poem is a sort of vision in which one man meets in hell the man he killed the day before. The poem ends with the peaceful "Let us sleep now".

Cross-referencing

Brooke was keen to go to war. He joined up as soon as war was declared, but died having never fought at all. Owen served in the trenches, where he suffered shell-shock. He was awarded the Military Cross and was killed only a few days before the Armistice in 1918. The two men's different experiences of war are clearly reflected in their poetry.

◎ *Make a list of all the main differences between the poetry of Brooke, Sassoon and Owen.*

Differences and similarities

In "The Soldier" Brooke writes of the "laughter learnt of friends" as something important. In "Strange Meeting", Owen writes that one of the soldiers regrets that "by my glee might many men have laughed". Both poets value laughter in life.

Brooke's poems are full of youthful enthusiasm and patriotic ideas. The pathos in Owen's poems lies in the fact that all these ideas have been wasted. Think about the attitudes of both poets to war and how these attitudes are conveyed through their poems.

Like Brooke, Owen uses words such as: "old", "weary", "sick", "dirty", "dreary". Notice the difference in effect. Owen uses them to write about the horrors of war – his dirt and dreariness belong to the filth of the trenches, not the England he left behind.

Can you find other similarities in the language and writing technique of the two poets?

⍰ *Think about the subject matter of "Peace", "The Soldier", "Dulce Et Decorum Est" and "Strange Meeting". In what ways are they different?*

World War I Poetry

Practice Questions

Write about the similarities and the differences between the poems of Brooke and Owen. You should consider:

- what the poems are about
- the different attitudes to war.

Following an argument

In your exam you might be asked to trace the argument of a poem. To prepare for this you should:

- **read** the poem several times
- **brainstorm** it, writing down as many points as you can

With these points in mind, go through the poem, stage by stage, to find out how the poet has presented his argument.

 Re-read and brainstorm "Digging". Write down your points. Think about what the poet has to say directly to you.

Tracing the argument

This poem opens with a picture of the writer at work. He feels very comfortable doing what he's doing (the pen is "snug"). He also feels that being a writer makes you very powerful. He imagines his pen is a gun.

The noise of digging attracts his attention: "Under my window, a clean rasping sound". As the poet looks at his father's backside bent over the ground, he calls to mind memories of him digging and the poem shifts in time to "twenty years away".

The poet notices several things about the way his father works. He tries to capture the actual feel of digging by using **alliteration**. This emphasises the cutting edge of the spade:

buried the bright edge deep.

Heaney leaves the word "deep" to the end of the line to show that the spade goes in a good way. He emphasises his delight by using more alliteration:

Loving their cool hardness in our hands.

 Re-read lines 6-15. Write a paragraph explaining how Heaney portrays his father digging.

A second major time shift takes place and Heaney starts to write, with pride, of his grandfather:

My grandfather cut out more turf in a day
Than any other man on Toner's bog.

The events of the poem are made more vivid by the recollection of an incident from Heaney's childhood:

> Once I carried milk in a bottle

The detail he introduces makes it all the more real:

> Corked sloppily with paper.

Heaney uses alliteration again to emphasise his grandfather's skill:

> heaving sods
> Over his shoulder

Sharp consonants are used to bring out the actual sound of the digging:

> Nicking and slicing neatly.

List the similarities in the portrayal of Heaney's father digging and his grandfather digging.

The way Heaney recreates the sounds and feeling of digging are essential, because the poet is recalling early memories. If you as the reader can feel what the poet felt, then you can appreciate what it meant for Heaney.

The next stanza uses more vivid sounds to recreate the act of digging:

> the squelch and slap

and:

> the curt cuts of an edge.

Heaney feels he cannot follow in the family footsteps. He writes:

> But I've no spade to follow like them.

The poem comes full circle, returning at its conclusion to the poet sitting waiting to write. The pen is no longer a gun, but a spade with which Heaney decides to dig. Heaney is now in harmony with his father and grandfather.

> **! REMEMBER**
> Look for what the poet suggests through the use of language – in images, symbols, rhyme and rhythm.

Practice Questions

By comparing his work to the work of his father and grandfather, what do you think Heaney is suggesting about:

- the pleasure to be found in the sound of poetry
- the way a poet works
- the importance of the past

Write a few sentences on each topic.

Heaney

Poets sometimes write accounts of their experiences that reveal how they feel about the things they describe. The poet may state their **moral** viewpoint – whether they think something's right or wrong. Usually however, the poet suggests possibilities. When reading a poem, you have to make up your own mind.

◎ *Re-read "The Early Purges." The poem looks at cruelty and suffering and asks if they are a necessary part of life.*

Expressing views

Heaney uses three **voices** to present his point of view.

The first belongs to himself as a young child:

   I was six when I first saw kittens drown.

The next voice is that of a farm worker, Dan Taggart:

   Sure isn't it better for them now?

The final voice belongs to the poet as a grown man:

   But on well-run farms pests have to be kept down.

REMEMBER
Underline words and phrases that show the poet's attitude.

The three voices express three attitudes towards cruelty:

■ the young child is horrified

■ Dan Taggart thinks it's just a part of farming

■ the adult poet seems to recognise the practical necessities

⁇ *Do you think the last voice is saying what Seamus Heaney actually believes?*

Using emotive language

Words which make us feel strongly about a subject are known as **emotive** words. Writers generally use them to persuade you to a particular point of view. Look closely at the language to see how the child's view is presented:

■ a frail metal sound
■ their tiny din was soon soused
■ glossy and dead
■ mealy and crisp

■ soft paws scraping like mad
■ they were shiny on the snow
■ three sogged remains

(?) *What does each phrase make you feel about the death of the kittens?*

(◎) *Write a sentence about each phrase.*

Now look at what Dan Taggart says. He calls the kittens "the scraggy wee shits" and asks "Sure isn't it better for them now?"

Which of the following words do you think best describe his attitude?

cruel   indifferent   heartless   mean   practical   ruthless   considerate

(?) *How do you feel about Dan Taggart's words and actions?*

In the fifth stanza Heaney writes about death on the farm by simply stating what the farm labourer did ("trapped", "snared", "shot"). Notice how matter-of-fact these duties seem to be.

In the final line, however, Heaney tries to appeal to the reader's sympathies by using emotive language. He states that the "tug" was "sickening", and the hen was "old".

Next comes the poet's adult voice. He states simply that "living displaces false sentiments". He is saying that his feelings as a young child are to be forgotten. They were "sentimental" and they prevented him from seeing the world as it really is. They were "false". It is only people in towns who think farming is cruel:

"Prevention of cruelty" talk cuts ice in town.

Reminding us of Dan Taggart, he now speaks of "bloody pups" and argues that "on well-run farms pests have to be kept down".

(!) **REMEMBER** Watch out for emotive words and phrases.

(?) *Does Heaney really mean this? How can you tell?*
Look for evidence in the poem.

Practice Questions

1 What does Heaney mean by "well-run" farms? Is a "well-run" farm the only type of farm? Is it necessarily the best type of farm? Perhaps the poet may have in mind another type of farm where there is no cruelty. What do you think?

2 What is the central issue of "The Early Purges"? Write about it, showing the different views towards this as explored in the poem. How does Heaney use language to influence the reader?

46

Poetry often deals with unfamiliar situations and feelings. Through reading a poem closely you can learn a lot about other people's lives and experiences. Often you have to think carefully about what lies below the surface of a poem in order to fully understand it.

 Re-read "Mid-Term Break". Remember that this poem is based on Heaney's own experience.

Relating to unfamiliar experiences

Not everybody who reads this poem has been to a boarding school or knows what a sick bay is. Fewer still will have experienced the painful loss of a brother or sister. Nevertheless, there are many points to which we can readily relate.

Heaney's picture of school is not too far removed from life in a state-run school today. Bells ring whichever type of school you go to. What is unusual about these bells is that they are "knelling". They sound sombre, setting the mood for what is to follow.

Revealing hidden feelings

Lines 4-13 describe the young boy's homecoming. The only feeling described is his embarrassment at the old men standing up to shake his hand.

How do you think the young Heaney might have felt about:
- *his father crying*
- *Big Jim Evans*
- *the baby in the pram*
- *the strangers*
- *his mother's sighs*
- *the difference between his father and his mother*

Why do you think these feelings are not described?

REMEMBER In the exam, you will need to show that you have thought about what lies beneath the surface message of a poem.

There is a sense of restraint in this poem, as though the feelings are being deliberately held back, lying just beneath the surface, perhaps becau~ are still too difficult and too painful for Heaney to express openly. ~~~se of restraint is reinforced by the arrival of the body which is described in a very distant and impersonal way:

> At ten o'clock the ambulance arrived
> With the corpse, stanched and bandaged by the nurses.

The exact time is given and the body of his brother is referred to as "the corpse", almost as it would be in a news report.

Symbols

The final seven lines of the poem describe how Heaney went to see the body of his young brother the following morning.

(?) *Think about the following phrases:*

- *Snowdrops and candles soothed the bedside*

- *Wearing a poppy bruise*

- *No gaudy scars*

What do you associate with snowdrops and candles? What do they symbolise?

Why is the bruise described as being like a poppy? What do poppies commemorate?

What does "gaudy" mean? Are scars normally described as being gaudy? Why do you think Heaney chose to use the word here?

Statements of fact

You have already noted how restrained the feelings are in this poem. This sense of restraint is, in part, created by the use of flat statements of fact, such as "I sat all morning in the sick bay".

(◎) *List as many simple statements of fact as you can find in the poem.*

It is only at the close of the poem that we learn, with the phrase "the bumper knocked him clear", how Heaney's brother died. This is stated simply, almost as a matter of fact. Does this mean there is no emotion behind it?

The poem finally ends abruptly with just two short phrases:

A four foot box, a foot for every year.

(?) *How effective do you find this as an ending?*

! REMEMBER
As a reader of poetry you need to form your own opinions.

Practice Questions

In "Mid-Term Break", Heaney writes about his brother's death.

1 What do you think Heaney's feelings towards his brother's death were?

2 How are these feelings brought out in the poem?

You must look closely at the language of poetry if you are to understand the poet's intentions. You also need to be able to:

■ write about the language

■ comment on its effectiveness.

Descriptive language

◎ *Re-read "Follower".*

Here Heaney is writing about his father and his relationship with him. Look at the way Heaney describes his father when he was younger:

■ His shoulders globed like a full sail strung

■ An expert

■   His eye
  Narrowed and angled at the ground,
  Mapping the furrow exactly

■ Sometimes he rode me on his back
  Dipping and rising to his plod

■ his broad shadow

Think about the first of these images. When Heaney's father is ploughing, his shoulders seem "globed like a full sail strung". The word "globed" not only suggests the way his shoulders were rounded and powerful but that they seem, to the young boy, as big and as important as the whole world. The use of the **simile** "like a full sail strung" reinforces the image of power and strength adding a suggestion of tautness and effort.

 REMEMBER
Look closely at the language in order to be able to comment on its effectiveness.

◎ *Look back to the list of things that Heaney says about his father. Explain what ideas each of these convey and how this is achieved through the use of language.*

Contrasting language

The image of the young Heaney contrasts sharply with the powerful images of his father.

  I stumbled in his hob-nailed wake.
  All I ever did was follow

and:

  I was a nuisance, tripping, falling,
  Yapping always.

(?) *What impression of the young Heaney is created by these words?*

His father's power and strength is not only conveyed through the descriptions of him. It is apparent also in his control of the horses and the soil. The horses "strained at his clicking tongue". This image conveys the idea that they are listening carefully and he is clearly in command. With "a single pluck" of the reins he is able to turn the horses round. The word "single" emphasises the extent of his control. The way the "sod rolled over without breaking" suggests that even the soil obeys him.

Change of tone

The last three lines of the poem take the reader by surprise. Without warning, the order is reversed. Now that Heaney is a grown man it is his father "who keeps stumbling behind" and "will not go away". In many ways their roles have been reversed.

(?) *Is the tone one of sadness, or resentment, or a mixture of both? Is Heaney sorry that his father has become dependent on him? What do the words "will not go away" tell you about Heaney's feelings towards his father?*

(!) R E M E M B E R Always look for evidence in the poem to support your answers.

Use of rhyme

The neat rhymes "sod/plod" emphasise the neat cuts his father makes with the plough. There are also several examples of half-rhyme:

- plough/furrow
- sock/pluck
- wake/back

These introduce a feeling of uncertainty, perhaps suggesting that, despite the father's power, there will come a time when things will change.

Practice Questions

1 Write two short paragraphs about the way Heaney describes his father, both past and present, in "Follower".

You should focus particularly on the words he uses.

2 "Follower" is about the relationship between Heaney and his father. It also makes us think about relationships in general. Do you agree? Give clear reasons for your answer.

50

In exams you are often asked to refer to a number of different texts in your answer. You need to be able to select material from these and to make comparisons between them.

 Make a list of any features which you think are typical of Seamus Heaney. These may be to do with content or style.

◎ *Re-read "Storm on the Island".*

Try to find ways in which this poem is similar to, or different from, those you have already read. Look out for the following:

Alliteration

There are many examples of **alliteration** in "Storm on the Island". This technique is used to emphasize the sturdiness of the houses:

> we build our houses squat,
> Sink walls in rock and roof them with good slate.

The strength of Heaney's father in "Follower" was depicted in a similar fashion:

> His shoulders globed like a full sail strung.

Similar sounds

Heaney uses harsh consonants to give a cutting edge, as you have already found in "Digging":

> a clean rasping sound
> When the spade sinks into the gravelly ground.

This is also present in "Storm on the Island".

◎ *Find as many examples of harsh consonants as you can in "Storm on the Island".*

Conversational language

Another feature of Heaney's style is his use of conversational language. He keeps your feet firmly on the ground with his **colloquialisms**:

> Sure isn't it better for them now? ("The Early Purges")

> By God, the old man could handle a spade. ("Digging")

In "Storm on the Island" there are further examples:

- as you can see
- you know what I mean
- we just sit tight

 R E M E M B E R As you are studying the poems of a particular poet it will help you to note down what you think are the most typical features.

Simple statements

Heaney often states things quite simply. Look at the following opening lines:

I sat all morning in the college sick bay ("Mid-Term Break")

I was six when I first saw kittens drown ("The Early Purges")

In a similar way "Storm on the Island" opens quite ordinarily:

We are prepared.

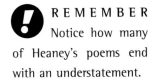

REMEMBER
Underline similar styles of language in your texts.

51

Effective descriptions

Heaney conveys powerful images through his use of language:

Like wet gloves they bobbed and shone ("The Early Purges")

The cold smell of potato mould, the squelch and slap
Of soggy peat ("Digging")

His shoulders globed like a full sail strung ("Follower")

In what ways is the storm described in "Storm on the Island"? How effective is this description?

Understatement

In "Storm on the Island" the gale is battering the houses but the poet reduces the force of the attack. He states that they were bombarded "by the empty air". His conclusion reduces the threat to a "huge nothing".

This use of understatement is typical of many of Heaney's final lines, like:

A four foot box, a foot for every year ("Mid-Term Break")

The final line forces the reader to think. In "Mid-Term Break" the abrupt ending raises questions about the poet's feelings towards his brother. "Storm on the Island" ends with "it is a huge nothing that we fear". Most of the poem is taken up with the picture of a storm, but this fear is reduced to a "nothing". Why? What kind of a storm is this? Is the poem really about our fears? Are they really as terrifying as the storm seems to be? Or are they, like the "empty air", nothing to worry about?

The conclusions, like the poems themselves, are thought-provoking.

REMEMBER
Notice how many of Heaney's poems end with an understatement.

Practice Questions

1 Refer to "Storm on the Island" and two other poems. How does Heaney use conversational language? What does this add to the poems?

2 Show how "Storm on the Island" contains similar features to those found in the other four poems studied. Remember to refer to the texts in detail.

Practice exam questions – literary texts

Try the following questions for yourself. Before reading the bullet points which follow each title, try to plan the essay for yourself.

Practice Question 1 – Macbeth

Consider the relationship between Macbeth and Lady Macbeth in the Banquet Scene. Compare it with their relationship as seen in Act 1 Scene vii.

! REMEMBER
Make sure you bring together points of similarity and difference.

In Act III Scene iv:

■ Lady Macbeth plays the concerned hostess who reminds Macbeth of his duties ("You do not give the cheer")

■ she tries to excuse her husband's behaviour ("My lord is often thus/ And hath been from his youth")

■ she tries to shake him out of his fear by taunting him about his vivid imagination ("This is the air-drawn dagger which, you said,/ Led you to Duncan")

■ Macbeth tries to justify his behaviour ("If I stand here, I saw him")

■ by persisting in her criticism she persuades Macbeth to confess his weakness ("I have a strange infirmity, which is nothing/To those who know me")

■ Macbeth is amazed that his wife is unmoved by the Ghost's presence ("When now I think you can behold such sights/ And keep the natural ruby of your cheeks")

■ she feels the source of his troubles is lack of sleep ("you lack the season of all natures, sleep")

In Act I Scene vii:

■ Lady Macbeth persuades her reluctant husband to murder Duncan. She taunts him (Macbeth: "We will proceed no further in the business"; Lady Macbeth: "Was the hope drunk wherein you dressed yourself?")

■ she criticises his manhood ("When you durst do it, then you were a man")

■ she tries to shock him into following her advice by using violent imagery ("I would while it was smiling in my face have pluck'd the nipple from his boneless gums,/ And dash'd the brains out")

■ when Macbeth appears uncertain about their plan she encourages him

("We fail!/ But screw your courage to the sticking-place")

- she does the planning ("his two chamberlains/ Will I with wine and wassail so convince")

- she tries to convince him that they are invincible ("What cannot you and I perform")

- Macbeth is impressed by her ability ("Bring forth men-children only")

- Macbeth is finally convinced and becomes interested in the details of the operation ("When we have mark'd with blood those sleepy two")

- finally he decides to take his wife's advice about concealing his real intentions ("False face must hide what the false heart doth know")

Practice Question 2 – Blake

Show how rhyme and rhythm play an important part in one of Blake's poems.

"The Tyger" by William Blake.

- Short lines give the poem pace to drive along the argument

- rhyming couplets help to tie ideas together (bright/night, skies/eyes)

- repetition of "and" drives the poem to its climax

- lines of monosyllabic words slow the pace and emphasise the meaning ("What the hand dare seize the fire?")

- use of foregrounding to hammer home ideas and emphasise Blake's questioning of the creator/creation ("What immortal hand"/ "What dread hand?")

- lines made up of chiming half lines ("What dread hand? and what dread feet?"/ "What the hammer? What the chain?")

- rhythmical emphasis on "Dare" in the final line highlights the shift in meaning from the last line of the first stanza

Practice Question 3 – World War I poetry

*Look carefully at two poems by Rupert Brooke, "Peace" and "The Soldier."
How differently does Brooke see England in these poems? Explain how the
poet reveals the differences.*

In "Peace" Brooke sees England as a land:

- which has been avoiding its responsibilities ("Wakened us from sleeping")

- where society was decadent ("a world grown old")

- which had lost its sense of values/idealism ("sick hearts that honour could
not move")

- where men had lost their manhood ("Half-men")

- entertainment was sordid ("dirty songs and dreary")

- men had no sense of responsibility to their country ("the little emptiness of
love")

In "The Soldier" Brooke idealises England, thinking of it as a country:

- which brings up its men in the right way ("A dust whom England bore,
shaped, made aware")

- which can make foreign countries into better places, even in death ("In
that rich earth a richer dust concealed")

- whose influence is felt even after death ("Gives somewhere back the
thoughts by England given")

- which allows peaceful values to flourish ("gentleness/ in hearts of peace,
under an English heaven")

In "Peace" Brooke has used:

- the language of prayer

- images of weakness contrasted with youthful idealism ("sick hearts"/
"swimmers into cleanness leaping")

- words are paired within the line to reinforce the meaning ("grown old"/
"cold and weary")

- the use of "and" gives the poem a feeling of continuity and takes the
reader along to the climax ("And all the little emptiness of love")

In "The Soldier" Brooke uses:

- the sonnet form to give the poem a classical dignity

- personification ("A dust whom England bore, shaped, made aware")

- images of paradise to idealise England ("dreams happy as her day")

- the regular rhyme scheme and rhythm which show the poet's confidence in his beliefs

- soft sounds to create an atmosphere of peace and contentment ("Her sights and sounds; dreams happy as her day")

Practice Question 4 – Heaney

In "Digging" what does Seamus Heaney have to say about the relationship between his skills and those of his father and grandfather?

- skills of Heaney and his father and grandfather, though different in many ways, do have some similarities.

- the poet's tool is his pen ("The squat pen")

- powerful weapon ("snug as a gun")

- father works rhythmically as does the poet writing in verse ("Stooping in rhythm")

- father produced things of beauty ("Loving their cool hardness")

- father and grandfather were skilled in their trade ("By God, the old man could handle a spade")

- grandfather had a reputation for his ability ("My grandfather could cut more turf in a day...."/ Heaney won the Nobel Prize for Literature)

- Heaney decides to use his pen as a spade to dig with, to unearth ideas/poems/language ("I'll dig with it.")

Non-fiction texts

Non-fiction texts are texts which are not poems, stories, novels or plays. They include newspapers, magazine articles, information leaflets, advertisements, biographies and autobiographies, letters and diaries, travel writing and reference books.

They are written to **inform**, to **persuade**, to **give advice** or to **describe**.

What skills do I need?

You are expected to:

- **extract information** from texts
- **distinguish** between fact and opinion
- **follow and explain** the writer's arguments
- **select material** according to purpose
- write about the way in which the information is **presented**
- consider how **effectively** the information is presented

How can I improve my reading skills?

REMEMBER Refer to the text frequently to support your answers. You must give as much evidence of your reading as you can.

In order to do well in exams you need to be a very efficient reader. The first thing to read in an examination is the question or task set, so that when you tackle the reading material you are reading with a very clear purpose.

You should read a text once so that you have a general idea of what it contains. Don't worry if you do not understand or remember everything the first time you read it.

The second time you read the text you'll be reading it to look for a particular piece of information needed to answer a question. This is known as **scanning**.

REMEMBER You'll find it helpful to underline the relevant parts of a text to help you answer an exam question.

How can this unit help me?

This unit can help you by explaining the skills in detail and by giving you clear examples and practice activities. At the back of the book there are answers to the test questions so that you can check your progress. Good luck!

Non-fiction texts are all around us in the form of adverts, leaflets, information sheets, newpapers, junk mail and many more items. In order to get familiar with this type of text, try reading some of the non-fiction texts which you see around you. You can also try to work out what techniques their writers have used to get their information across in an interesting and appealing way.

Study these texts and work out why they were written and in what sort of publication they would appear.

A

How to Vote

This leaflet tells you how you can still vote even if you are unable to go to your polling station on election day. Providing there is a good reason why you cannot vote in person, you can apply to vote by post or proxy.
(A proxy is someone who votes on your behalf).

For example:
- if you will be away on holiday (in the UK or abroad);
- if your work takes you away from home;
- if you are ill or in hospital.

Some people qualify to vote by post or proxy for a longer period of time, not just at one particular election.

You will need to say on the application form whether you want to vote by post or by proxy.

If you want vote by post you must give the full address to which your ballot paper should be sent. It must be in the United Kingdom. Postal ballot papers are normally sent out about a week before polling day.

If you want to appoint a proxy to vote for you, he or she must be:
- willing to vote on your behalf;
- a British citizen or citizen of the Commonwealth or the Republic of Ireland; or for local government and European Parliamentary elections, a citizen of the European Union;
- old enough to vote and legally allowed to vote.

B

Castle: A fortified defensive building. Its name derives from the Latin word *castellum,* a small fortified place. The castle underwent many changes in its history to counteract the development of increasingly powerful weapons. In the early middle ages a castle consisted of a simple building on a mound of earth surrounded by a wooden fence (the motte and bailey castle), a design later copied in stone. The simplest stone castle, such as the White Tower of London, is called a keep or donjon. Later designs became more complicated, involving extensive outworks of battlemented towers and walls (curtain walls), e.g. Caernarfon Castle in Wales. As they could not be built to withstand cannon fire castles lost their military usefulness; some, such as Windsor Castle, were converted into large houses.

C

YOUR HEALTH

with Dr Kay Hadley

● ● ● ● ● ● ● ● ● ● ● ● ● ● ● ● ● ●

How can I heal all my burns?

Q I cook a lot and am prone to small burns on my hands and wrists. Is there any way that I can soothe these naturally and, perhaps, get them to heal more quickly? *J. Smith, London.*

A The most important thing after you have burnt yourself is to run cold water over the burn. This takes much of the heat out of it and helps to limit its severity. For maximum benefit, keep the burn under cold running water for several minutes and apply ice, too.

While minor burns can be treated at home, large or severe injuries should be looked at by a doctor, just in case you need medical treatment.

Pure essential oil of lavender can be soothing. Apply it several times a day while the burn is healing. This will help it heal quickly with the minimum scarring.

Taking certain nutrients may also help healing. Zinc and vitamin C are probably the most important. I recommend you take 30mg of zinc each day and 1g of vitamin C twice a day to promote skin healing.

Extracting information

It's important to learn how to extract information quickly and efficiently. This is the first step towards doing well in exams that test your reading skills.

Follow these simple steps

● Read through the questions so that you know what you are looking for.

● Read through the whole text once and try to work out what it means. Don't worry if you don't understand everything the first time you read it.

REMEMBER
Underlining key words and phrases as you read will help you to write a good answer.

● Re-read the text quickly looking for the particular bits of information asked for in the exam questions. This is known as **scanning**.

● As you are reading, underline the pieces you need in the text.

Read the following text. It is taken from a leaflet about dental care for children. There are many separate pieces of information in it. Here's one:

"The most important place to clean is the join between your gums and teeth."

◎ *Find 5 more pieces of information. Write them in the form of a list – do not copy long pieces of information from the text.*

KEEP TEETH HEALTHY

HAVE FEWER SUGARY FOOD AND DRINKS

Having lots of sugary foods and drinks is bad for teeth, and it's even worse eating and drinking them off and on during the day.

If you want to have foods and drinks which contain sugar, save them to have with meals. Eat or drink them at one go.

Some foods such as cheese and unsalted or plain peanuts can help protect your teeth from decay. So these make good snack foods.

Use a small-headed toothbrush with medium bristles and change your toothbrush every 2–3 months. The most important place to clean is the join between your gums and teeth. This is where most of the bugs are found. Your toothbrush bristles should go over this join. Gently move the toothbrush in small circles then flick it out. Gently brush the biting surfaces of your teeth too, using the same circling movement. You don't have to scrub hard.

If you're not sure that you're brushing your teeth properly, tell your dentist next time you go. If your gums bleed when you brush your teeth, it's even more important to brush them regularly – the bleeding is caused by bad gums and brushing will help.

It will take several minutes to give teeth a really good clean, not just a few seconds.

BRUSH YOUR TEETH REGULARLY AND PROPERLY

Brush your teeth properly at least twice a day to remove the plaque – in the morning and before you go to bed.

Find a toothpaste that you like. Fluoride will help make your teeth strong. Remember – toothpaste doesn't clean your teeth, you still need to brush them.

VISIT YOUR DENTIST REGULARLY

Practice Questions

Read the newspaper article about Jazzie B and answer the questions below.

The Guardian, Monday 6 October 1997

The difference a day made Jazzie B

Jazzie B was born in north London, of Antiguan parentage. He co-founded Soul II Soul in 1982 and now owns a recording studio, record label and fashion line. He lives in London with his partner and two children. Soul II Soul's sixth album, Time for Change, was released last month.

The day was Sunday April 6 1997 – the day my dream came true. Jazzie B playing Wembley in front of 75,000 people – and I scored. It rectifies everything in my life.

In the seventies, when I was at school in Holloway, it was everyone's childhood dream. But you never could really imagine yourself at Wembley coming down the tunnel, never mind scoring more or less from the halfway line and watching the ball go into the net. I used to want to be a PE teacher, because being a football player wasn't something I thought I could do – there were not many black players at that time and my icon was Clyde Best, even though he played for West Ham and I was an Arsenal boy. He was the only one I could really relate to.

I have a big family and as the youngest was treated as a kind of mascot (I was so spoiled as a little kid) and when I scored, everything went through my mind really fast. I remember thinking: "Did it go in?" and then: "Wait till I tell my brothers, they are not going to believe this."

I was playing in a celebrity match before the Coca-Cola Cup final. When I'd got the letter asking me to play, I was running round the studio like a kid. Things like that get me truly excited.

It really was unbelievable. I felt like I did when we had our kids, I was walking on a cloud. It was the winning goal, so they gave me the ball and I had to do a lap of honour and everything. It was mental.

I remember my teachers saying to me: "You must work hard and play hard" and it's true. Put a bit of hard work and belief into something and it becomes a reality; when you lose sight of your belief, it fragments. I've had number one albums, done all sorts of things, but nothing beats playing football at Wembley.

Annie Taylor

1 What did Jazzie B want to be when he was at school?

2 Which does he think is better – having a number one album or playing at Wembley?

3 What did he do when he got the letter asking him to play in the celebrity match?

4 What is the name of Soul II Soul's sixth album?

5 Find and write down 3 pieces of information about each of the following:

■ Jazzie B's job

■ his childhood

■ the celebrity football match

Don't copy long pieces of information from the text.

Fact and opinion

Facts are things we can prove and things we know for certain are true. **Opinions** are personal – they are what a person believes. They may not be true for a wide range of people.

Fact or opinion?

Look at this advertisement.

(?) *Is this fact or opinion?*

The use of the number might make you think that it is a fact. But how do we know that the offers are fantastic?
This is somebody's **opinion.**

Now what about this one?
This is a **fact** because the statement can be proved.

Look at the key points highlighted in the passage below. As you can see, there are examples of both facts and opinions.

60

REMEMBER Don't be tricked by numbers. They can appear in both facts and opinions.

Easy pickings on the street

Have you ever watched the police moving a car that's causing an obstruction? Or asked for help when you've inadvertently locked yourself out of your car? If so, you'll know just how easy it is for someone who knows what to do, and has the right equipment, to get into your car.

1 As a part of our car tests we check the security of doors, windows, boot or tailgate, bonnet, glovebox, steering column lock, petrol filler lock and sunroof.
Here we tell you what we've found. It adds up to a sorry picture for car owners and a disgraceful one for car makers.

5

6

Buying a car is, for many people, the second most costly purchase they make in their life - second only to buying their own home. And yet car makers seem to put car security pretty low on their list of priorities.
We can't publicly blow the whistle on the specific design weaknesses we find in doors and locks, for fear of worsening the crime rate. But the makers know the problems as well as we do. They should be making doors more secure, protecting the ignition system and fitting an alarm system as standard (or, at least, offering it as an option). The car makers must take more action to combat the sky-high car crime figures.

1 is a **fact** because this could be checked and proved to be true.

2 is also a **fact** because this could also be checked.

3 is an **opinion** because it is the personal belief of the writer.

4 is also an **opinion** because this is a suggestion and not something which can be checked.

5 and 6 are **opinions** because they refer to feelings or beliefs and not known facts.

REMEMBER Underline key words and phrases in the exam before you decide if they're facts or opinions.

LOOK OUT FOR words which signal opinions, such as:

seem   appear   suggest   might   should   could   would

These all suggest possibilities rather than something that can be proved.

LOOK OUT FOR **emotive** words or phrases, such as "it adds up to a **sorry picture** for car owners and a **disgraceful** one for car makers."

These are words which are intended to appeal to your **feelings** or **emotions**. People often use them when they are expressing an opinion.

! **R E M E M B E R**
A fact can be proved. An opinion is a personal belief.

⊙ *Have a look at a newspaper article. How many emotive phrases can you find? Write three of them down.*

Practice Questions

Car Alarms

How they raise the alarm
The alarms set off either the car's horn or their own sounder – a horn or siren. Using the car's horn might be a bit of a risk if the thief is familiar with the car – he could open the bonnet and cut the horn connections. A siren is a distinctive sound – people nearby might take notice more quickly. Flashing headlights and indicators, are likely to raise eyebrows, especially at night.

Does it immobilise the car?
Many alarms also knock out the car's ignition. This is obviously a worthwhile protection – if a thief knocks out the horn he may still be unable to drive off.

What triggers the alarm?
Alarms can be triggered by vibrations made by a thief before the door is opened, a door being opened, or by something inside (the thief's movement, or by the engine being started, for example). The sooner the alarm goes off, the better.

How persistent is the alarm?
Many of the alarms go off only for a limited time after some sort of disturbance – sensible as it avoids too much unnecessary rumpus. Most importantly, all the vibration alarms stopped after a while if accidentally triggered off. But a cut-off could be bad if it left the car exposed after the thief's initial attack – some alarms stopped even though the door was still open.

Security against alarm being switched off
The alarm's switch is a weak point. Perhaps the weakest is a key switch outside the car that can be picked easily. Many alarms are worked by a flick switch inside – totally vulnerable once found, though the thief would have to brazen out the noise while looking.

How convenient?
Simple flick switches are quite convenient. A few systems worked with the car's ignition switch – even more convenient.

False alarming?
A car alarm that goes off unnecessarily, because the car is buffeted by gusts of wind, say, can drive people nearby to distraction. Some alarms were more prone to accidental triggering than others.

1 The extract above contains both facts and opinions. Can you find five examples of each?

2 Write them down in two separate lists headed FACT and OPINION.

Following an argument

Being able to follow an argument is a skill you need to answer exam questions.

Following an argument simply means understanding and explaining the points of view presented in a text.

One writer might argue that the minimum age for legally buying fireworks should be raised due to an increasing number of firework accidents among young people. To make this argument the writer might include **facts** about the dangers of fireworks as well as his own **opinion** of the irresponsible behaviour of young people.

REMEMBER Always read the whole text through and underline key words.

How to follow an argument

- Read the whole passage.

- Underline the key words and phrases which best express the writer's argument.

- Work out the different stages of the argument.

REMEMBER You can check if you understand an argument by seeing if you can tell someone else what the text is about.

Read through the article below which presents one woman's view about putting her mother into a residential home for old people.

Underline words and phrases that reveal her different points of view. List the difficulties she has in arranging care for her mother. Then list the positive results of putting her mother in a home.

LOOK OUT FOR the turning point in the article "I started looking at homes..."

Is it fair to put Mum in a home?

Mum is 88, and she'd lived in west London for 53 years before she had a fall in April this year, and was taken into hospital. I'd always worried that if she needed more care, I couldn't cope at home. She needs lots of help, but wouldn't want me to give up my career. It would be impossible for her to live with us – our house is too small.

But all the guilt and the social pressures are horrendous. A lot of people are shocked that I could even think about putting my mother in a home.

Mum hates hospitals, and her mental state was deteriorating when she first went in. She had another fall in hospital, but then she was transferred to a terrific rehabilitation ward.

The social workers there said Mum's needs would be assessed to see what sort of care she required. I was scared she'd need nursing care – a lot of people in nursing homes are very confused, and I was worried that Mum would be put in a room full of mad people.

I started looking at homes, and the one I'm hoping Mum will go to looks excellent. We're still waiting for the final assessment and for the council to agree that this particular home is right for Mum.

Before she had her fall I knew she needed help, but I couldn't persuade her to take it. Now I know she'll be well cared for, her meals will be cooked for her and she'll have people around her, and we've actually become closer as a result of her fall.

In the next example – a report from the *Guardian* newspaper – the writer comments on various points of view related to the changing world.

While this article clearly presents various points of view about the changing world, it also suggests further arguments about:

- the role of the monarchy
- the place of technology
- gender issues and equal opportunities

Behind every argument there are often further issues which are not stated directly but are implied. These are known as **implications.**

Queen, 71, bemoans trials of modern life

Jamie Wilson on varied reactions to the monarch's reflections

She may have her own internet site, and was jetting around the world before most people had ever been airborne, but yesterday the Queen confessed that she found it hard to keep up with the modern world.

The 71-year-old monarch, who is in Pakistan on the second day of her state visit, told the country's parliament: "I sometimes sense that the world is changing almost too fast for its inhabitants, at least for us older ones."

Her comments drew support from a number of her more elderly subjects. Veteran writer and broadcaster Ludovic Kennedy said he agreed entirely: "What she has said is absolutely right. For old dogs like us, new tricks are simply unacceptable."

Mr Kennedy, 77, continued: "The world is changing so fast we just can't keep pace with it.

"That is something older people have to accept."

Romantic novelist Dame Barbara Cartland, 95, echoed the Queen's sentiments, saying: "The world is changing too fast. The Queen is right, we need to get back to the way we were in the past.

"We need to get back to a previous age, where men behaved like gentlemen and women were women and not so busy building their careers. I think that is what the Queen was trying to say and I agree with her."

However, Tony Benn, the 72-year-old Labour MP, felt one change was long overdue.

"The one thing that has not changed in my lifetime is the monarchy. If we could move into the next century with an elected head of state I would feel optimistic," he said.

But it was not all pessimism at the fast rate of progress. Betty Felsted from St Albans, a 70-year-old member of the Women's League of Health and Beauty, said that old

people were sometimes blinded by science but that should not stop them from trying to keep up. "Just before I retired I learned how to use a word processor and I have no problem with video recorders or washing machines: I just read the instructions and get on with it.

"I always have a go at anything that comes along."

But Age- Concern spokesman Margaret McLellan was sympathetic to the Queen's remarks, saying: "Many elderly people will feel the same way as the Queen.

"Feeling too old to catch up with the modern world can begin when people are as young as 40 or 50, and it is a feeling which gets worse as people get older."

Practice Questions

1 What point is the Queen making about modern life?

2 How does Ludovic Kennedy support and extend the Queen's point of view?

3 Look again at Barbara Cartland's views on the changing world. In what ways are her arguments different from those of Ludovic Kennedy?

4 What does Tony Benn's contribution add to the argument?

5 In what way do Betty Felsted's arguments disagree with some of the previous statements?

6 Which out of all the views presented in this article is the closest to the views of the Queen? Explain why.

Collating material

Collating material means gathering together information from different texts.

Now you have learned how to follow an argument, you can have a go at gathering the bits of information you need from a range of texts.

Study the following texts about animal rescue.

(?) *What do you learn about the work of the RSPCA from the appeal and the article?*

◎ *List 10 points about the work of the RSPCA, using the phrases underlined in both texts to help you.*

Here's the first point to help you:

"The RSPCA gives first aid and essential medication to rescued animals."

> **REMEMBER**
> For this task you will be using the skill of scanning which you have already revised.

Just £8 makes the difference between life and death

- £8 goes towards first aid and essential medication given to a rescued animal.
- £8 will help the RSPCA build and run animal shelters where abandoned animals find safety; where the beaten and tortured receive veterinary care; and where the neglected and ignored find love.
- £8 helps to pay the cost of starting a new RSPCA inspector's training. Right now, we have 305 inspectors.

All of this has to be paid for by donations. Please help us and use the donation form attached. Tomorrow will be too late for victims of cruelty.

Please send your donation to this address:
*'Fight Against Cruelty' Appeal,
RSPCA, FREEPOST, BRISTOL BS38 7LQ*

Make cheque or postal orders payable to RSPCA.

No stamp needed, but, if you use one more of our funds go to help animals.

*RSPCA inspectors –
the front line against cruelty to animals*

We Britons are proud of our reputation as animal lovers. In every town and city, there are countless people concerned about the welfare of creatures great and small. Unfortunately, that's not the whole story. The reality of life in any industrial country is that wildlife usually comes off second best in encounters with humans. Cars, pollution, building projects and downright cruelty all regularly claim casualties.

The RSPCA is doing what it can to redress the balance. The society has three specialist wildlife hospitals which treat injured or orphaned animals, always with the objective of returning them to their natural habitat. The latest, Stapeley Grange Wildlife Centre, just outside Nantwich, Cheshire, has been overwhelmed with work since opening at the end of 1994.

WILD REFUGE

The more we encroach on nature, the more work we create for wildlife sanctuaries. Chris Hulme reports.

The hospital was previously a private house, with seven acres of grounds, surrounded by farmland. The handsome Victorian building was bequeathed to the RSPCA by Cynthia Zur Nedden, who died in 1991, on the proviso that it would be used to relieve the suffering of animals. Since being converted and extended, the house now includes an operating theatre, a pre-op room where animals are prepared for surgery and an isolation area for animals carrying diseases that can be passed on to humans.

There are also special rooms for washing oiled sea birds, a nursery for orphans and fledglings, and several generic pens which can be used as and when the need arises.

'We deal with about 4500 animals and birds a year,' explains Michele Grayshon, deputy manager. 'Most of our patients are brought in by RSPCA inspectors but sometimes members of the public come knocking on the door.'

Study these texts about endangered species and the problems they face.

£17.50 PER ADOPTION AND RECEIVE OUR

ACT NOW
A TRULY HUMANITARIAN GIFT

ADOPT A HUMPBACK WHALE

and protect them 365 days a year.

When you adopt one whale you'll be helping all whales.

Humpback Whales are extremely susceptible to the hazards of whaling, hunting, fishermen and natural calamities such as being beached in their annual migration between Canada and the Caribbean. Many of our female whales that are up for adoption are mothers that have had several babies. You can choose to adopt one of these female humpback whales with her baby for just £17.50 per adoption. Or you can choose a single female or a strong male. The choice is yours.

Whatever you decide upon, you can be certain in the knowledge that your money will be spent directly on the protection and survival of these magnificent gentle giants.

! REMEMBER Underline the key points as you study the texts.

Adoption Papers

NAME: *Kinyanjui*   AGE: *13*   SEX: *Male*

Adopt a rhino, before it's too late

Kinyanjui is a black rhino. Not so long ago – only as far back as the seventies – he would have been one of 60,000 in Africa. Now, a monstrous trade has decimated these numbers. A staggering 95% of black rhinos have been cold-bloodedly butchered for their horns – worth three times the price of gold on the black market.

Today, Kinyanjui is one of only 434 of these magnificent beasts left alive in Kenya.

A grim picture? In fact, Kinyanjui and his fellow black rhinos are on the increase, thanks to WWF. Since we began supporting the Kenya Wildlife Service project in 1992, the population has actually risen. But the numbers are still desperately low – which is why we need your help.

Stop the slaughter, adopt Kinyanjui for yourself or a friend

By adopting Kinyanjui for just £2 a month you can help us protect him from the horrors of illegal poaching. To thank you, we'll send you a Certificate of Adoption, a photograph of Kinyanjui and regular updates on his progress. If you could find it in your heart to adopt this remarkable animal you'd be helping us to save more than his life alone. You'll be supporting our goal to see 600 healthy black rhinos in Kenya by the turn of the century, and you'll be helping us to ensure that every endangered rhino throughout Africa and Asia stands a chance of staying alive. The future of rhinos everywhere could depend on you.

Practice Questions

1 What problems do endangered species face? List 6 points using both texts.

Here's the first point for you:

"The numbers of black rhinos in Africa have been greatly reduced – in the seventies there were 60,000 black rhinos in Africa."

2 What similarities are there beween the way the two advertisements have been written? List 4 points using both texts.

Identifying the purpose of a text

So far you have looked at an advice leaflet, magazine articles, charity appeals (or adverts like the RSPCA one) and newspaper cuttings. Each text is different depending on its **form**, its **purpose** and its **intended audience**.

! REMEMBER Underline key words in the text that will help you to decide its form, purpose and audience.

In order to identify its **form** you need to ask yourself:
What is it? Is it an advertisement, an article, a travel brochure, a diary extract or something else?

In order to identify its **purpose** you need to ask yourself:
Why was it written? Was it written to inform, explain, instruct, entertain, advise, persuade, or for some other reason? Does it have more than one purpose?

In order to identify the **audience** you need to ask yourself:
Who was it written for? Was it written for an adult, teenager or child or a combination of these? Was it written for someone with a particular interest? What else can you work out about the intended reader?

◎ *Read the pieces of text on the next page, then write an answer for each of the texts under each heading. The first one is done for you.*

	FORM (what is it?)	PURPOSE (why is it written?)	AUDIENCE (who is it written for?)
A	a recipe	to instruct	anyone wanting to cook a quick, cheap meal for one
B			
C			
D			
E			

A

Savoury Eggs   *Serves 1*

A cheap and tasty variation on the bacon 'n' egg theme; makes a good, quick supper.
For a change, cooked sliced sausages or slices of salami can be used instead of bacon.

Preparation and cooking time: 25 minutes.

1 small onion
1 small eating apple
1 rasher of bacon
2tsp cooking oil or large knob of butter (for frying)
Salt and pepper
1/4 tsp sugar
2 eggs

Peel and slice the onion. Wash, core and slice the apple. Derind the bacon and cut into 1/2 in (1.25cm) pieces. Heat the oil or butter in a frying pan over a moderate heat. Add the bacon, onion and apple, and fry, stirring occasionally, until soft (about 5 minutes). Stir in the salt, pepper and sugar. Remove from the heat. Break the eggs into a cup, one at a time, and pour on top of the onion mixture. Cover the pan with a lid, and cook for a further 3 to 5 minutes over a very low heat, until the eggs are as firm as you like them.

B

Saved – thanks to RSPCA supporters

Without the help of animal lovers like you, the RSPCA would be powerless in the war against cruelty and suffering. See for yourself how your donation can help save the lives of animals who have known only fear, pain and suffering.

Locked in a room for weeks without food, 10-year-old retriever Oliver was just half his recommended weight when the RSPCA found him. The vet said Oliver would have been dead within two days if we hadn't rescued him. Now fully recovered thanks to the dedicated care of RSPCA staff, Oliver has finally found the loving home he deserves.

C

IMPORTANT SAFEGUARDS

When using electrical appliances basic safety precautions should always be followed, including the following:

1. Read all instructions.
2. Do not touch hot surfaces.
3. To protect against electric shock do not immerse cord or plugs in water or other liquids.
4. Do not insert metal objects, knives, forks or similar implements into the bread slot.
5. Close supervision is necessary when any appliance is used by or near children.
6. Do not use any unauthorised attachments with your toaster, they may be hazardous.
7. Unplug from outlet when not in use and before cleaning.
8. Do not cover your toaster whilst it is hot or in use.
9. Appliance should not be used if the supply cable is damaged or dropped causing visible damage.
10. The use of accessory attachments not recommended by the appliance manufacturer may cause injury.
11. Do not use outdoors.
12. Do not let cord hang over edge of table or worktop or touch hot surfaces.
13. Do not use appliance for other than intended use.
14. Bread may burn. Therefore toasters must not be used near or below curtains and other combustible materials. They must be watched.

SAVE THESE INSTRUCTIONS

D

now she's old enough to look after her own smile – what about yours?

Return to nursing
Full or part-time flexible hours

Giving up a few years to look after a child has its own special rewards. But when they no longer need all of your time, returning to work can be a daunting prospect. Whatever your reason for taking time out, don't worry – your nursing skills are always valuable, whether they were learned 10 months or 10 years ago. If you've had a break from nursing, for however long, we can offer you one of the best ways to get back in.

E

Telephone: (01203) 7746962
Fax: 01203 59687

Hillcrest Garden Products,
Freemantle Estate,
Coventry,
CV7 5TH

26th July, 1995

Our reference: JCG/SM/14

Mr K.Gillham,
27, Fairfield Road,
Scunthorpe,
SC6 BN4

Dear Sir,

Thank you for your letter of 17th July. Whilst we are naturally most sympathetic concerning the unfortunate events which involved our RM14 Rotary Lawnmower, we cannot agree that Hillcrest are in any way responsible nor can we entertain your claim for compensation.

You're probably already aware of the different ways the texts we read in our daily lives are presented.

You can easily spot the different styles of, say, an advertisement, a recipe or a newspaper report.

In exam answers you must comment on the effect and impact of the appearance, or **layout**, of texts as well as their content.

Headlines

The use of bold lettering, capital letters and an exclamation mark makes the headline appear dramatic and eyecatching.

In this headline the question mark gives you something to think about.

The pound sign and the number attract your attention here.

Different sorts of print

Often a text will use a range of types of print to draw attention to particular points.

This typed letter opens with a handwritten style. One reason for this is that it makes the appeal more personal and direct.

action for blind people
....
14-16 Verney Road London SE16 3DZ
Telephone 0171 732 8771 Fax 0171 639 0948

Helping Blind & Partially Sighted people since 1857

Dear friend

I wonder what you will say in answer to this letter; I shall await your reply with some anxiety, for if our letters go into the waste paper basket we shall be unable to continue our many services for the benefit of those who are blind.

68

Logos

Companies and charities use **logos** as a visual image which you can identify whenever you see them.

B B C RADIO 1

Charts and diagrams

These are used to present complex information in a simple and easy-to-read way.

 Look in a newspaper or magazine and see if you can find 3 charts or diagrams. Think about the impact they have on the reader.

Photographs and illustrations

Visual images have a powerful impact on the reader. We often look at a picture before we read the text. The way pictures are used can set the tone for a text. For example, cartoons can create a jokey effect, while photographs can add a sense of realism.

Practice Questions

Oxfam
FREEPOST (OF 353)
274 Banbury Road
Oxford OX2 7BR

Help them build a future free from hunger and disease

How does Oxfam make your £2 work so hard?

How can we possibly make just £2 do so much?

The answer lies in the effort, the determination, and the ingenuity of the people we help.

Oxfam doesn't walk into a Third World country with ready-made solutions, or quick-fix answers. We work alongside local people, and help them work out solutions that suit their individual circumstances.

The projects Oxfam supports are always carefully monitored, so that money isn't wasted, and worthwhile lessons can be applied elsewhere.

Oxfam supports 3,000 projects in over 70 countries worldwide.

...for just £2 a month.

**Your £2 a month will help these people in their daily struggle to help themselves.
Please complete the coupon inside.**

1 How many different types of print can you identify?

2 Why do you think the print is of varying sizes?

3 What impact do you think is made by the pictures?

Evaluating the language of a text

In the last unit you looked at the way text is presented. This unit will help you to identify different types of language used in texts and comment on them.

Types of language

Dramatic or emotive language

> **Hospitals face crisis over fall in blood supplies**

This is used to attract the reader's attention – especially in newspaper headlines. **Emotive** language is language which is intended to arouse strong feelings. In the example (left) the word **crisis** attracts your attention and encourages you to read the article.

Imperative or directive language

Imperatives and **directives** are words which give us instructions or orders. They are used to appeal directly to the reader and to make the message very clear. In the example (right) the word **discover** is being used as an imperative.

> **DISCOVER** Your FAVOURITE days out in **CHESHIRE**

Alliteration

> **Ringway rumpus**
> POLICE were called to Manchester Airport

This is where writers use the same letter to start several words in a headline, like in the example (left). It's another way of catching your attention.

Questions

Questions are used by writers to get the reader involved directly. They have the same effect as the use of directives – they make you think the writer is talking to you personally. The article on the next page starts with the question "*How green are you?*" This has the effect of involving the reader straight away.

Colloquial language

REMEMBER
Make a checklist of types of language to look out for in a text.

This is the name for everyday speech. Colloquial language is informal. It is used to convey ideas in a particular way and to make it easy for the reader to relate to the text. In the text "How green are you" on the next page, some examples of colloquial speech have been underlined for you. The whole effect of this text is that of a friend having a conversation with you.

◎ *Look through a newspaper or magazine. Find three examples of alliteration, emotive and colloquial language.*

How green are you?

Hands up if you have recently done any of the following:
- thrown a glass bottle in the rubbish bin;
- left the tap running while cleaning your teeth;
- poured cooking oil down the drain;
- flushed cotton wool down the loo;
- left the fridge door open while paying the milkman;
- thrown away plastic carriers from the back of a cupboard;
- heated the oven to bake a solitary spud.

Yes, me too. On the other hand, I do recycle bottles, cans and paper, and take clothes to charity shops, so I thought I was doing pretty well, until I started working on this supplement.

Who can put their hand on their heart and honestly say that they always make the greenest decisions about their home?

Practice Questions

Friday October 24, 1997

Community News

Ninja peril of Black Lake

Dumped terrapins decimate wildlife

An exotic pet which grows from the dimensions of a 50p piece into a plate-sized monster is causing havoc among wildlife after being dumped illegally in a Wilmslow pool.

There are thought to be dozens of American reared terrapins – left-overs of the Ninja Mutant Turtle craze – in Black Lake on Lindow Common.

The 12in-diameter creatures gobble up insects, newts, frogs and even baby water birds. Experts say that unless the terrapins can be curbed local wildlife will be devastated.

The problem began when the terrapins were dumped after they became too big to handle in household aquariums.

The wily reptiles are proving difficult to catch. So far, they have dodged all efforts at trapping.

The terrapins – *trachemys scripta elegans* – have found the lake in the 43-acre wildlife reserve of scientific and special interest an ideal breeding ground. Even in their native North America, where they are known as red-eared sliders, they are a major problem, producing up to 23 eggs a year.

Macclesfield council countryside officer Richard Doran says anyone dumping the reptiles in the lake can be fined up to £5,000.

"Everything was all right until the Mutant Ninja craze came along," he said.

1 Find and write down three examples of emotive and colloquial language.

2 Give three examples to show how the writer has used language to attract and keep the reader's attention.

Writing skills

What will I be asked to do?

In the exam you'll be asked to produce writing that argues, persuades or instructs, or that explains, informs or describes.

You may be asked to write different things such as letters, leaflets, articles, reports or speeches. These tasks will probably be linked to the topics of the non-fiction texts that were used in the questions that tested your reading and understanding.

Whichever tasks you choose, you'll need to write for a particular audience in a way that gets your message across.

What skills do I need?

You are expected to:

- plan your work so that the finished piece of writing is **well organised**
- match your writing to your **audience and purpose**
- organise your ideas into sentences and **paragraphs**
- **vary** the length and style of your sentences
- use a wide range of **vocabulary** which is suitable for the task
- present your work **clearly and neatly** using legible handwriting
- use correct **punctuation**
- **spell** correctly

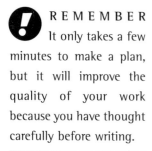 **REMEMBER** It only takes a few minutes to make a plan, but it will improve the quality of your work because you have thought carefully before writing.

Planning your writing

Examiners give credit for work which is well structured and logical, so you should spend time planning your work before you start writing. Then you can decide what you are going to say, how you are going to say it and in what order you will present it. You can make a simple plan – just a few key words or sentences can help you to organise what you want to say.

Presentation

Different types of writing need different types of **presentation.** For example, there are certain ways of setting out a letter.

If you are writing an article think carefully about a suitable headline.

Block capitals, underlining and different types of writing can all be used for emphasis if your task is an advice sheet or leaflet, for example.

Making an impact

The best way to do this is to match your content, vocabulary and sentence structure to the needs of your audience and the purpose of your task.

Paragraphs

Dividing your ideas into paragraphs helps the reader to follow your argument. This is very important when writing in exams.

Generally, you should put all your ideas on the same topic in one paragraph. If you stop writing every few minutes to read what you have written, it should be easier to see if you need to begin a new paragraph.

Punctuation

Punctuation helps the reader to make sense of what is written. When you are working alone you'll find it helps to read your work aloud after you have written it. This will help you to decide where to put commas, full stops and question marks, etc. In an exam you need to think ahead. Plan each sentence carefully **before** you start writing.

Spelling

Correct spelling is crucial in writing exams. Take time to revise spellings before the exam and make use of English textbooks, which often have spelling rules written at the back. You could even buy your own book of spelling rules.

Make a note of words you often get wrong and make a special effort to learn them. Pin them up near your desk so you can see them as you do your revision.

Writing under exam conditions

- Always spend a few minutes reading the questions. Make your choice carefully so that you know exactly what type of writing is required.

- Don't begin to write until you have made a plan.

- Try to think about each sentence before you write it.

- Don't forget to keep on reading your work through as you are writing.

- Leave a few minutes at the end of the exam for reading over your answers, and make changes and corrections where necessary.

! REMEMBER
Read through your work after you have written each paragraph. That way you are more likely to spot mistakes and avoid repeating yourself.

Writing

Matching writing to an audience

The **audience** for a piece of writing is the person or people you are writing for.

When you are writing it is very important to match your **vocabulary, content** and **sentence structure** to the needs of the reader.

Look at the piece of writing below which is aimed at children. You can see that the vocabulary and the sentence structure are simple so that they can easily be read and understood.

Bicycles

The first bicycle was a <u>sort of</u> hobby-horse on wheels. It had no pedals so you had to push it forward like a scooter. It was impossible to steer.

You could steer this bicycle by turning the handle-bars. But you still had to push it along with your feet.

This was one of the first bicycles with <u>pedals</u>. <u>Pedalling</u> was very hard work. The <u>pedals</u> went backwards and forwards and drove the back wheel.

bicycle compared with children's toys

informal language

use of You to involve the reader

vocabulary repeated - only one idea in a sentence

 REMEMBER Use facts to inform your reader, use **you** to address the reader and ask questions to involve the reader.

◎ *Using your own ideas write a short paragraph to explain one of the following to a younger child:*
- *how to make a piece of toast*
- *how to make a cup of tea*

Study the extract on the next page which was written for a teenage audience. What do you notice about the vocabulary and sentence structure now? They have become more complicated to match the needs of older readers.

◎ *Using the information in the article "What makes a good friend" on the next page and your own ideas, write a paragraph for a PSE text book entitled "Choosing a friend".*

What makes a good friend?

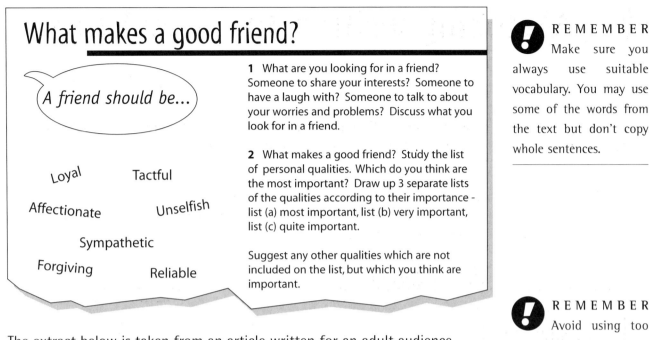

A friend should be...

Loyal   Tactful

Affectionate   Unselfish

Sympathetic

Forgiving   Reliable

1 What are you looking for in a friend? Someone to share your interests? Someone to have a laugh with? Someone to talk to about your worries and problems? Discuss what you look for in a friend.

2 What makes a good friend? Study the list of personal qualities. Which do you think are the most important? Draw up 3 separate lists of the qualities according to their importance - list (a) most important, list (b) very important, list (c) quite important.

Suggest any other qualities which are not included on the list, but which you think are important.

> **! REMEMBER** Make sure you always use suitable vocabulary. You may use some of the words from the text but don't copy whole sentences.

> **! REMEMBER** Avoid using too many simple sentences when writing for adults or teenagers.

The extract below is taken from an article written for an adult audience about teenage gambling. Some of the language is clearly targeted at the adult reader. We have underlined two such examples for you. Can you find others?

One-armed bandits

For many teenagers the <u>lure</u> of the fruit machines is irresistible. The combination of noise, lights and cash incentives make them an <u>attractive form of escapism</u>. However, many experts now see them as increasingly responsible for the growing number of teenage gamblers. 'Fruit machines are a form of hard gambling,' says Dr Emmanuel Moran of the National Council of Gambling. 'They are compulsive and habit forming.'

In fact, a survey, carried out by the National Housing and Town Planing Council, suggested that more than 300,000 British teenagers spend their school dinner money on fruit machines. Over 130,000 are stealing money from their parents to finance their obsession.

Practice Questions

Write a short article aimed at alerting parents to the dangers of teenage gambling.

Here are some ideas to help you.

- *It is believed that the problem of teenage gambling is growing...*
- *Fruit machines are becoming attractive to teenagers because...*
- *Gambling is habit forming...*

Writing

Writing for a purpose

The **purpose** of a piece of writing is the reason why it is being written. It is important to be aware of the purpose for a piece of writing before you begin. Then you can match your ideas, vocabulary, style and presentation to this.

Different purposes in writing

Writing to persuade

REMEMBER When writing to persuade, include lots of emotive language to make your description more exciting. Emotive language will also help you to make your point more directly.

Read the text below written to persuade people to visit the Albert Dock in Liverpool. The text mixes some facts with lots of opinions and uses carefully chosen words to persuade the reader that this is a good place to go to. Some of these words have been underlined for you. See how many more you can find.

The Albert Dock
Liverpool

Exciting shopping!

For shopping that's different, there is nowhere quite like the Albert Dock.

■ Undercover malls house scores of small, individual shops and brightly coloured coster carts displaying an amazing range of merchandise.

■ From toys to treasures, candy to clocks, books to baseball caps, the Dock's got the lot!

■ Fashion-seekers of all ages are well-provided for, with shops selling ladies, men's and children's fashions. Accessories? You'll find no shortage of

jewellery, scarves, bags and fragrances to go with that new designer outfit.

■ Souvenir hunting? The Dock can hardly be bettered. There's a <u>staggering</u> range of Beatles mementoes along with items commemorating those other local heroes, Liverpool and Everton Football Clubs. And in between there's everything from a picture postcard or guidebook of the Albert Dock to ships' clocks and other reminders of the city's <u>proud</u> maritime past. "Shop at the Dock" – it's all part of the <u>irresistible</u> Albert Dock experience!

Writing to argue

REMEMBER When writing to argue, include some facts to convince the reader.

Read the text on the next page on the topic of banning fireworks. Two opposing points of view are presented here. We have labelled the features of this type of writing for you to study.

reader involved directly

facts to support argument

Fireworks: time for a total ban?

YES Let's bring an end to the dangers of fireworks, and impose a total ban on the things once and for all. This newspaper has already highlighted how a new law banning the sale of dangerous fireworks to children is being ignored by some shop owners in Greater Manchester. Even organised displays aren't safe, as was proved last night, when people, including children, were injured at a display in the West Midlands.

Every year in the build-up to Bonfire Night, Postbag publishes letters from people who are sick and tired of hearing fireworks being left off in their area weeks before November 5. Youngsters terrorise old people and those with pets.

Every year people are maimed and even killed by fireworks, despite all the government's efforts to warn of the dangers. Thoughtless idiots will always ignore the warnings, and innocent people will be hurt, unless we ban all fireworks now.

NO Talk of banning all fireworks is an over-reaction. It is true that people are hurt by them, but nothing can be made completely safe these days, not even crossing the road! For many years fireworks and bonfires have brought lots of enjoyment to generations of people in this country. It is one winter's night when everybody gets out and about and has fun. Banning fireworks would put a lot of people out of work, for one thing. And you could hardly ban fireworks without forbidding people to build bonfires. How on earth could such a ban be imposed?

Last night's display was an unfortunate accident, and people were hurt, but it was a one-off. The vast majority of such displays are safe, and there is no earthly reason why they should not continue to be so. Let us not deny children the pleasure that Fireworks Night can bring.

rhetorical question

final opinions clearly stated

emotive language

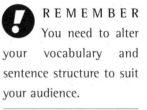
REMEMBER Aim to make the reader share your views by using the words "we" and "us".

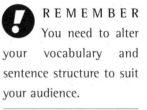
REMEMBER You need to alter your vocabulary and sentence structure to suit your audience.

Writing

Writing to instruct

This type of writing is different from writing that persuades or argues. When we write to instruct, ideas should be expressed simply and clearly without using emotive language or personal points of view, just as in the article below.

Water saving ideas

- Take showers instead of baths – a bath uses 80 litres of water compared to 35 for a shower. Power showers tend to use as much as a bath, so use the economy setting.
- Fix dripping taps – they can waste a surprising amount of water over time.
- Turn off the tap while you're brushing your teeth. Most of the water we use this way goes straight down the plughole!
- Save washing-up to do in one go. Washing one mug under a running tap uses a litre of water. Fill a bowl to rinse plates and crockery after washing – don't just leave tap water running. Save this water to pour on the garden afterwards.
- It's estimated that one third of our domestic water is flushed down the loo – each flush uses about 9 litres of water.
- Use washing appliances carefully. A washing machine uses up to 80 litres per cycle, and a dishwasher up to 35 litres.

Practice Questions

1 Write a short article, based on an attraction of your town or of a place you have visited, for a local newspaper. Include bold headings to attract the eye of your readers.

2 Write an article for a school magazine in which you either agree or disagree with a ban on fireworks. Aim to make the audience share your point of view by using the words WE and US.

3 Using the ideas in the article on water saving ideas, write a paragraph for a local council leaflet giving instructions and hints to householders on the subject of saving water.

Writing letters

In the exam you may be asked to write a letter for a particular purpose – for example, to complain, to persuade or to express an opinion.

Look at the following letters taken from newspapers and magazines. Each letter has been written for a different purpose.

REMEMBER Identify the issue in your opening paragraph. Explain your position clearly, giving reasons why you feel the way you do.

Letter 1

This letter has been written to express an opinion. We have identified some of the features of such a letter for you. Study them carefully.

> ### Dear BBC Vegetarian Good Food
>
> My girlfriend is a vegetarian and she buys your magazine. I'm not a veggie, but I've noticed you carry advertisements for vegetarian dog food in your publication.
>
> I think it's cruel to force your own preferences on a poor animal that can't choose for itself. I own a dog and I only have to watch him eat to see how much he loves meat. I can't believe he'd be half as fit and healthy without it.

first paragraph identifies the issue

expresses and develops opinion

REMEMBER Use emotive vocabulary to emphasise your points.

Letter 2

This time the letter has been written to **persuade** the reader to adopt the same opinion as the writer. The distinguishing features of this letter have been labelled for you.

> ### Quiet, please
>
> A year ago the Royal British Legion wrote asking for your readers' support for a two-minute silence at 11am on November 11. Over the past two years, the nation has demonstrated its strong sympathy with the idea.
>
> So we write to seek your support again – for a two-minute silence on Tuesday November 11. The legion hopes that everyone in the country will have, or be offered, the opportunity to pause for two minutes silent reflection at 11am.
>
> We look particularly to parents and teachers to respond to our call again this year. Our children have not known the horror of war, save perhaps through news pictures from Bosnia, the Gulf or elsewhere. We should ensure that they understand the value of peace and security by explaining to them the meaning of remembrance. This year, the Spice Girls have agreed to help.
>
> Graham Downing,
> National Chairman,
> Royal British Legion, London

first paragraph identifies the issue

direct appeal to the reader – use of 'we' and 'your'

emotive language

Letter 3

This is a letter of **complaint**. Study the labels and explanations carefully so that you can learn to recognise the features of a letter like this.

If the Government can make a fuss about children taking holidays in term time, it should try to stamp out the greater menace of bullying.

While your education correspondent was reporting a purge against holiday absentees, Jessica Davies urged us all last week 'for sad Kelly Yeoman's sake', to stand up against the bullies.

But it's no good calling on the general public to take individual action. Heads and their staff are the first to get a whisper of what goes on and parents of bullies and their victims are usually the last to know.

The Government seems blind to anything other than the education system pouring information into children's heads, whether they are capable of absorbing it or not.

opinion clearly expressed in first paragraph

reference to other people's opinions

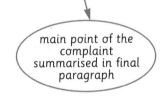

main point of the complaint summarised in final paragraph

Driving the limit down

THERE can be really no reasonable argument against Britain's drink driving limit being brought into line with the law in the rest of the European Union. It will mean bringing down the legal limit from its current 80 mgms of alcohol per mls of blood to 50 mgms. That, for some people, means the equivalent of one pint of beer.

For some people – and that's the trouble. While even a shadow of uncertainty is allowed to remain – and one's body chemistry is an uncertain science – there could be the temptation, even among law-abiding people (hard core drink drivers are another matter entirely), to take a risk.

Those who argue that the only logical blood alcohol limit that would remove all uncertainty is zero, have a case. Any other limit rather contradict urgings: don't drink and drive.

Writing

(?) What issue would you write to a newspaper or magazine to complain, persuade or express an opinion about?

Practice Questions

Read the letter above on the topic of Britain's drink driving limit. The writer of this letter is in favour of bringing down the level of alcohol permitted for driving.

■ What are your views on this issue?

■ Write a reply clearly stating your views.

Leaflets and advice sheets

Writing to inform, explain and describe

A **leaflet** is an information booklet that is usually printed on folded paper in an easy-to-read format. The aim of a leaflet is to present **information** on a particular topic in an eye-catching way. As well as giving information, a leaflet can also explain and describe. Leaflets can give information on a wide variety of subjects ranging from holidays to health. **Presentation** is the key to making sure that a leaflet will appeal to its audience. The use of effective headings, pictures, clear explanations and short but interesting descriptions also have a place.

Study the leaflet below where we have highlighted the essential features of presentation for you.

 Write a leaflet about a local place of interest or a theme park. A visit to your local information or tourist office should provide you with plenty of useful material for this task. In your leaflet you should aim to include interesting titles or headlines, pictures, explanations of activities and descriptions of the place.

! REMEMBER Include a variety of lettering and use bold headlines.

! REMEMBER Use diagrams, pictures and bold headings to vary the presentation.

Discover
the Fascinating Story of
Working Life
at Quarry Bank Mill....

A unique experience and a great day out – with an array of major tourism awards to prove it.

From Cottage Industry to Industrial Revolution, Quarry Bank Mill demonstrates in a fascinating and practical way how cotton became King.

Discover what daily life was like for the hundreds of mill workers through a series of dramatic reconstructions, live demonstrations and hands-on displays.

The Styal story started back in 1784 when Samuel Greg harnessed the waters of the River Bollin to power his mill for the manufacture of textiles.

Today many original features remain just as they were over 200 years ago giving a unique view of our industrial heritage.

Since the Mill and its estates were donated to the National Trust the site has been fully restored as Europe's largest working textile museum, with all round family appeal.

...and explore
the Beauty of
Styal Country Park

topic clearly identified in headline

explanation of activities

descriptive language

emotive language

Advice sheets/leaflets

These are written with a very specific purpose in mind: to give advice on a particular topic. The language and presentation of an advice leaflet is adapted to suit the level of the audience.

Advice leaflets contain lots of facts which are often presented in an attractive way to make sure that the audience can understand them easily.

 Study the following advice leaflets to see if you can work out the purpose and audience for each one.

! REMEMBER Short, relevant sub-headings summarise the content of particular sections of text.

! REMEMBER Avoid using too many long paragraphs in a leaflet.

A GETTING INTO GOOD HABITS

● Aim to use less of everything. Stick to instructions and hold back on that extra squirt.

● Ask yourself whether the sink really needs another clean or whether clothes can be aired rather than washed.

● Cleaning products work better in soft water, so you can use less. If you live in a hard water area, use a softener.

● Do you really need individual cleaners for the different parts of your home?

● Stop buying aerosols, even if they don't contain CFCs.

B

Most parents, quite rightly, worry about their children trying drugs. They want to know the risks and what to do if they suspect their child is using drugs. But – as many teachers, hospital staff and police officers will tell you – alcohol can cause just as many problems for young people.

1,000 children under the age of 15 are admitted to hospital each year with acute alcohol poisoning.

Around half of pedestrians aged between 16 and 60 killed in road accidents have more alcohol in their blood than the legal drink drive limit.

In 1994, 57,800 people were found guilty or cautioned for drunkenness. The peak age of offenders was 18.

This booklet is about encouraging young people to be sensible about drinking – not a word that young people use themselves much. So you may need to find other words to explain the advantages of treating alcohol with respect.

It's time to talk to your child about sensible drinking.

Children are aware of alcohol at an early age. They can recognise different types of drink. Most children have their first alcoholic drink between the ages of 10 and 13. This introduction usually takes place at home without their parents' knowledge. They help themselves from the family drinks cupboard or at family occasions when adults aren't watching.

By the age of 13 to 16, young people may be passing cans or bottles round a group somewhere away from adults like a park or at parties. The group may drink quickly because of fear of being found out. It doesn't take much alcohol for youngsters of this age to get drunk.

From the age of about 16, young people may start going to pubs. Drinking often means getting drunk. Young people say getting drunk makes them feel good, more self-confident, more 'themselves'. They say it's a way of escaping the pressures at home and school. They say everyone else drinks, so why shouldn't they?

Writing

Practice Questions

Using the information in text B above and your own ideas, write an advice leaflet aimed at a teenage audience about the dangers of alcohol. Use colloquial (informal) language to appeal to your audience.

Writing reports

Reports usually appear in newspapers. They tell readers about recent events which have happened locally, nationally or internationally.

People often read newspapers quickly so the style of presentation needs to be snappy. The reader's attention is grabbed by the **headline.** The first paragraph contains the story's main points. The following paragraphs continue the story and usually give answers to the questions *who, what, where, when, why, how.*

Report style

■ They usually refer to what people have said.
■ They may include a brief description of people involved in the story.
■ They are written in the past tense because they refer to events which have already taken place.

Study the report below. We have labelled the features of report writing for you.

headline   past tense

Kaylee sets the pace for a heartfelt celebration

KAYLEE Davidson will be celebrating a very special event on Tuesday – the 10th anniversary of her donor heart.

The lively youngster from Washington, Tyne and Wear who loves to dance, run and play was just five months old when she became the youngest child in Britain to have a successful heart transplant. Yesterday Kaylee was guest of honour at a party in Newcastle for her and 50 other heart transplant children, alive thanks to donor families and surgeons at the city's Freeman Hospital.

Her mother Carol, 29, now vice-chairman of support group Heart Transplant Families Together, said: 'I can't believe 10 years have gone by. Kaylee is a normal little girl and she lives life to the full.'

main point of story in first paragraph

brief description

use of direct speech

❗ REMEMBER Include clear headlines and summarise the main part of the story in the first paragraph.

◎ *Write your own news report based on one of the following:*
■ *the decision by a local council to sell playing fields to make way for a motorway*
■ *gales and torrential rain which have caused damage to houses and flooding*
Use some, or all, of the features labelled above in your report.

Sometimes reports in newspapers use a particular event to raise points about matters of general concern. These reports give some information about a recent happening, but the main emphasis is on making the reader aware of the general issues. The article below is a good example of this type of reporting.

Practice Questions

Read the report carefully and then answer the questions. They will help you to understand the way in which the report has been presented.

Hitting out

Should parents be allowed to smack their children? Emily Moore looks at the issues.

A 12-year-old boy won the right to go to the European Court of Human Rights in Strasbourg last week because his stepfather beat him with a garden cane when he was nine years old. The hearing may take two years – if the boy wins, smacking could be banned in Britain.

Does British law allow grown-ups to hit children?

Yes it does. Parents have the right to use what is called "reasonable chastisement" to keep their children under control (1933 Children and Young Person's Act). So, parents may hit them, but not hard enough to cause serious injury.

However in 1991, the British government did agree Article 19 of the United Nation's Convention of the Rights of the Child, which says children should be protected from all forms of physical or mental violence. The UN is "deeply worried" about British law which allows adults to hit children.

Do any countries ban smacking?

Physical punishment of children is illegal in Austria, Cyprus, Denmark, Finland, Norway and Sweden. Sweden banned it in 1979 and studies show that violence against children has declined in the 17 years since then.

Why do parents smack their children?

Most parents were smacked when they were children and some believe it is the best way to stop a child's bad behaviour. All children need to learn the difference between right and wrong – the question is, does smacking teach this?

1 What event is the starting point for this report?

2 What issue is raised in this report?

3 Where does the report use facts and figures to help the reader understand the issues?

4 How does the report draw the reader's attention to different aspects of the issue being discussed?

5 Using the information in the report above, write your own report on the topic of smacking children. You can also add your own ideas. You may wish to include some opinions from both parents and children.

Writing

Articles appear in magazines as well as newspapers. They could cover a wide range of topics depending on the audience and the purpose of the publication in which they appear. Some articles are written to give **advice**. Others are written to **inform** the reader.

Articles don't necessarily just report news. They can also be written to develop an argument or to present a particular point of view.

◎ *Read each of the examples on this page and the next and decide in each case who is the audience and what is the purpose.*

You can see that articles adopt a different tone according to the audience.

The vocabulary of the first text is informal, while the writer of the second text uses a few technical terms and facts and figures.

Look at the article on the next page where we have labelled the distinguishing features of article writing for you.

Hi-tech, low life

Do computers turn children into spotty, uncommunicative youths? Not always says **Bill O'Neill**

Your seven-year-old daughter is determined to prove that she's now big enough to be a nerd, too. She slips into the back room while the rest of the family is watching Blind Date, switches on the computer and keys in the password (cleverly stuck on the back of the machine so children won't find it).

You're not worried about her coming across an unsolicited invitation among your family e-mail to surf the Internet in search of a "hot new product, try me out", the sort of appeal that thinly disguises a new pornography site; you cancelled your subscription to the company that provided your connection to the Internet more than a month ago because the service was too expensive and getting on-line too unpredictable.

No, your real concern these days is the amount of time that the children spend in front of that damn machine; they seem to be at it all day in school, and then want to do the same in the evenings and at the weekends at home. It'll ruin their eyesight, make them even more uncommunicative than they already are and generally turn them into fat, spotty youths, fit only to be wrapped in an anorak.

How come no one else realises that computers are designed to appeal to the lazy streak, that's why children like using them so much? Don't give me all that guff about improved motor skills and budding entrepreneurs – it's games, games, games. Once a child has made it to the terminal, everything he or she needs to pass the time of day is just a finger tap away, without having to move. On the computer, you're in charge; and if things don't go your way, you can simply press the re-set button.

Wheels are a wonder of the world. Take a look at what they consist of: 32 thin steel wires; 32 brass nipples; a light alloy hoop; and at the centre of the whole thing, a hub. None of the component parts are very strong and all (with the possible exception of the hub), are bendable.
However, give these components to a good wheel builder and within an hour or two they can transform them into lightweight structures capable of supporting upwards of one hundred times their own weight.

Gee Mom, TV has made me American

By Sean Poulter
Media Correspondent

headline designed to catch interest of audience – here it uses humour

sue identified in first paragraph

opinion of expert

opinion of expert

use of facts and figures

range of views given

Children are watching so many American television programmes they are losing touch with British life, a watchdog warned yesterday.

Some have such a constant diet of Stateside shows that they believe 911 – the US emergency number – rather than 999 is the one to call in a crisis.

As well as alienating youngsters from their own culture, American TV does not instil the social values British programmes do, said Jocelyn Hay, from the voluntary watchdog Voice of the Listener and Viewer.

Home-grown shows are more likely to get children thinking about and acting on social issues, she told the group's conference in London. 'With American TV, what we are also losing is the social and educational values linked with British television, such as the children showing compassion and interest in other parts of the world,' she added. 'For instance, when they see something on Rwanda, they go back to school and have a jumble sale.'

An invasion of cartoon characters is also squeezing out high-quality children's drama and educational programmes.

Since 1981, cartoons on BBC and ITV have jumped from 10 per cent to around 33 per cent of programming. Yesterday, broadcasters were warned that the 'dumbing down' of children's programmes would eventually filter into general schedules.

Anna Home, who has just stepped down from running the BBC's children's output, said it is becoming harder to get good-quality children's drama on screen. Miss Home, who commissioned the controversial Teletubbies, said 'High-quality drama is under pressure because it is so very expensive.'

The conference heard that children prefer series such as EastEnders, Casualty and Friends to those specifically aimed at them.

At the same time, critics complained that violent cartoons shown on ITV on Saturday mornings – and other programmes such as the Power Rangers – are becoming dominant.

The squeeze on quality programmes was confirmed by the Broadcasting Standards Commission. Director of research Andrea Millwood-Hargrave said the explosion of satellite channels has unleashed a tide of American cartoons. There are now five satellite children's channels. As a result, programming aimed at youngsters has risen from 10,000 minutes in 1991 to 86,000 minutes in 1996.

ITV's Michael Forte said parents should take a bigger role in directing children's viewing. 'Cartoons are great, but not a solid diet,' he added.

Writing

Practice Questions

The article above claims that children are being given too many "easy" and unchallenging programmes to watch on television.

Write your own article in which you put forward your point of view on the type of TV programmes available for children OR teenagers.

Here's a test of the skills that you have learned so far. Answer the questions below. This should take you about one hour. Good luck!

Practice Question 1

! REMEMBER Don't forget to underline key words and phrases.

Read the advertisement below for Milton sterilising fluid.

Find and write down four facts and four opinions.

! REMEMBER Don't forget your check list for commenting on presentation: headlines, different types and sizes of print, and the use of photographs and pictures.

! REMEMBER There can be different types of language in the same text, e.g. emotive, informative, technical, colloquial.

One of these tomatoes is contaminated by E.coli

(If you can't tell which, don't worry.)

Food poisoning is on the increase.

E.coli bacteria have now been found not just on meat, but on the surface of fruit and vegetables too. (They'd been fertilised with contaminated manure.)

To make matters worse, certain types of E.coli have even developed a resistance to some antibiotics.

Isn't anything safe to eat any more?

The good news is, E.coli bacteria have a deadly enemy: Milton Fluid.

In fact Milton, when diluted with water and used as recommended, kills all germs.

No wonder more and more people are buying it, whether there's a baby in the house or not.

And they're using it not just on their fridges, kitchen surfaces and chopping boards, but also for rinsing fruit and salad vegetables.

Perhaps doing that sounds a bit odd, eccentric even.

If it does, why not try this test for yourself: following the instructions on the pack, rinse some tomatoes, grapes or other fruit in diluted Milton, then let them drain until the surface is completely dry.

When you come to eat them, you'll find that Milton hasn't even changed the taste at all. (Even though it will have killed germs by the million.)

Better still, fruit and veg rinsed in Milton stay fresh for days longer.

That's because Milton kills the bacteria that make food go off, as well as the ones that cause food poisoning.

Maybe it's not such an odd thing to do after all. More like common sense, in fact.

Especially when the alternative is just hoping for the best.

FAMILY PROTECTION FROM FOOD GERMS

Practice Question 2

Read the article "Beat the Bugs". List two ideas from this article and two ideas from the advertisement on the previous page which might give the reader anxieties about food poisoning.

BEAT THE BUGS

National Food Safety Week is June 9-16. Moira Whittle reports on the latest news

Cryptosporidium This parasite, present in farm animal faeces which are washed into the water supply by rain, produces a toxin that can cause stomach upsets. Since 1992, there have been between 3,574–5,705 confirmed cases a year in England and Wales.

Salmonella Chickens fed on non-sterile food in the early '80s passed the salmonella organism into their eggs. Today, there are 30,000 confirmed cases a year, and about 50 deaths. Poultry, meat and eggs are the largest source of infection. 'At risk' groups – the elderly, very young and those with reduced immunity – must not eat raw eggs, and should not eat poultry unless thoroughly cooked very recently.

E.coli Many strains of Escherichia-coli exist in the gut of mammals, causing gastro-enteritis. They spread

Most people know someone who's had a bout of food poisoning in the last year – not surprising when you consider the number of cases has quadrupled in England and Wales from 19,242 in 1985 to 82,041 in 1995. Why has this increase occurred? And what can we do to minimise the risks?

Experts put the rise in figures down to new procedures that boost food production levels and shelf lives, as well as to consumers who, now more aware, are more likely to report cases. Media scares have heightened consumer fears and with good reason. At the end of last year, 19 people died in Lanarkshire, Scotland, in a food poisoning outbreak caused by the lethal E.coli virus. Another scare hit the headlines a few months ago when north London residents were warned to boil up tap water before drinking it to guard against infection by cryptosporidium.

by causing diarrhoea in their hosts. However, the 0157 strain, first identified in the '80s, is unique because it produces a toxin that causes renal failure. Confirmed E.coli cases in England and Wales rose from 411 in 1994 to 792 in 1995 after screening techniques were improved. Last year, E.coli cases totalled 660.

Listeria First recognised about 15 years ago, this bacteria is relatively unaffected by low temperatures and can be present in soft cheeses, chilled ready-made meals and patés. It causes fever and flu-like illness, which may be mild, but it can cause serious neurological damage in unborn babies, so pregnant women need to take care. Listeria cases peaked at 290 in 1988 when 26 new-born and unborn babies died in an outbreak due to contaminated paté.

Practice Question 3

Compare the article on this page with the advertisement on the previous page and write about the different ways in which they inform and persuade you about the dangers of food poisoning.

In both pieces comment on each of the following:

- the language used
- the style of presentation
- the attitude to the reader
- your opinion of how well each text informs and persuades

Practice exam questions

Now that you've thought about how to argue, persuade and instruct in writing, you are ready to do some exam practice. Each of the questions below should take no more than an hour. Before you begin this section, have another look at the unit on writing skills.

Practice Questions 1

REMEMBER Always make sure your writing style is suitable for both your purpose and audience.

A. Write a letter of complaint to a holiday firm seeking compensation for a holiday that went wrong.
   In your letter you should comment on the travel arrangements, the accommodation, the food and the facilities and entertainments available at the resort.

B. Write a letter to a newspaper complaining about the way young people are portrayed in the press, which you feel gives them a bad image.
   In your letter you could draw attention to the involvement of young people in sport, community activities, charity work, travel overseas, their school work and other issues which you consider to be relevant.

C. Read the extract below. Write a letter to the editor of a newspaper expressing your opinion on whether smoking should be banned in public places.

Ban it in public places?

YES How much more evidence does the government need to hear before it bans smoking in public places once and for all? A new report has produced damning proof linking passive smoking with chronic ill-health in adults and children.

It is blamed for causing breathing difficulties in asthma sufferers as well as eye irritation, headaches, coughs, sore throats, dizziness and nausea. That is in people who don't smoke, but have to endure the effects of this filthy habit which inconsiderate smokers inflict on them.

If you go to north America you will see strict measures against smoking in public places, such as shopping malls, and it is about time we took a leaf out of their book.

Many people detest the odours of other people's cigarette smoke. Now there is incontrovertible evidence that it harms everybody's health. Ban it now.

NO The heath freaks have gone too far. Not content with telling us that almost everything we eat or drink is bad for us, they now insist on trying to stop the pleasure of people who want to enjoy a quiet smoke now and again.

Smokers are already being hounded out of many places. Many smokers aren't even allowed to smoke at work now – they have to stand outside on the pavement, in the wind and rain. It's ridiculous.

This is supposed to be a free country, and part of that freedom should mean being able to smoke if you wish. What will the fuddy-duddy health freaks want next – a total ban on smoking? Don't they realise how much smokers pay in taxes?

There are far more dangers in the amount of exhaust fumes fouling our land. The government should do something about that.

Practice Questions 2

A. Write an advice leaflet for students taking GCSE exams. Your leaflet should include advice on revision, how much and how often, how to cope with exam stress and how to prepare for the exam itself. You may also want to offer hints and advice on exam performance.

B. Write an advice leaflet for students in year 7 beginning their first day at secondary school. You may refer to your own school in particular or you may make your advice more general. Topics you should cover include finding your way around, having the right equipment, making new friends and overcoming fears and worries.

! **R E M E M B E R**
Think about presentation and attracting the reader's attention.

The Balance of Playground Power

■ One in five children in Britain is either a bully or a victim of bullying. Some researchers believe this is just the tip of the iceberg: they think more like 70 per cent of the school population is involved.

■ A pilot study of 4,000 primary schoolchildren for Kidscape, the children's safety group, revealed that 38 per cent had been bullied, and that bullying was one of children's main worries.

■ Male bullies outnumber female bullies three to one. Boys bully both sexes, girls generally tend to stick to their own sex.

■ There is a higher incidence of bullying in urban schools than in rural schools.

■ Statistics say 68 per cent of all school bullies will become violent adults. A bully has a 25 per cent chance of committing crime in adult life (the average is five per cent).

■ Strong links have been established between truancy, underacheivement and bullying.

Practice Questions 3

A. Read the extract above about bullying. Write an article to be read by parents giving them information and advice about this problem.

Use your own ideas as well as those in the extract.

B. Write an article for a travel magazine in which you describe the attractions of your local area. Make your area sound as attractive as possible by commenting on local beauty spots, places of historic interest, shops, sporting facilities, restaurants, cinemas and other places of entertainment.

! **R E M E M B E R**
Organise your ideas before you start writing.

! **R E M E M B E R**
Make your local area sound like a place worth visiting.

Practice exam questions

Suggested Answers

You'll see that these answers are for the reading section only. That's because the questions about writing and literary texts often ask you to write a piece of text using your own ideas or opinions, so there isn't any one answer we can give you. If you want to check your progress on the questions about writing or literary texts, you could ask your teacher to look at your answers.

Non-fiction texts (page 56)

Text A: a leaflet written to explain how to vote.
Text B: an encyclopedia entry to give information on castles.
Text C: an extract from a questions and answers letters page in a women's magazine.

Extracting information (page 58)

Dental advice leaflet:

sugary food and drinks are bad for teeth; it is best to have these only at meal times; cheese and peanuts make good snack foods; brush your teeth twice a day, in the morning and at night; use a small-headed toothbrush with medium bristles; change your toothbrush every 2-3 months; the most important place to clean is the join between your teeth and gums; use your toothbrush with a circular movement; spend a few minutes cleaning your teeth; visit your dentist regularly

Jazzie B:

1: Jazzie B wanted to be a PE teacher
2: playing at Wembley
3: he ran round the studio like a kid
4: Time for Change
5: *facts about Jazzie B's job*: he co-founded Soul II Soul in 1982; he now owns a recording studio, record label and fashion line; his sixth album was released last month.
Facts about Jazzie B's childhood: he went to school in Holloway; he was the youngest in a large family; he was spoiled when young; he wanted to be a PE teacher; his hero was Clive Best; he supported Arsenal.
Facts about the celebrity football match: it was played before the Coca-Cola Cup final; the date was April 6 1997; there were 75,000 people there; he scored the winning goal.

Fact and opinion (page 60)

Facts:

alarms set off either the car horn or their own sounder; many alarms also knock out the car's ignition; alarms can be triggered by vibration; many alarms only go off for a limited time; some alarms stopped even though the door was open; many alarms are worked by a flick switch inside; a few systems worked with the car's ignition switch; some alarms more prone to accidental triggering than others.

Opinions:

using the car's horn might be a bit of a risk; the thief could open the bonnet; people nearby might take notice; this is obviously a worthwhile protection; the sooner the alarm goes the better; sensible as it avoids too much rumpus; a cut-off could be bad; the alarm's switch is a weak point; simple flick switches are quite convenient.

Following an argument (page 62)

Difficulties:

social pressure, people were shocked; Mum hates hospitals; her mental state was deteriorating.

Positive results:

the home she will go to looks excellent; she will be well cared for; she will have all her meals cooked for her; she will have people around her; mother and daughter have become closer.

Questions
1. The Queen says it is hard for an older person to keep up with the modern world.
2. Ludovic Kennedy says it's difficult for old people to adapt to the fast pace of change in the modern world.
3. Barbara Cartland says we need to go back to the ways of the past.
4. Tony Benn questions whether or not a monarch is needed in the modern world.
5. Betty Felsted is 70 and does not have any problems in keeping up with the modern world.
6. Ludovic Kennedy because he says: "What she has said is absolutely right".

Collating material (page 64)

1. 95% of black rhinos have been killed; rhinos are killed for their horns; 434 rhinos left in Kenya; humpback whales are threatened by whaling, hunting fishermen and natural calamities; they can be beached during migration.

2. Both adverts give the reader facts explaining why animals are in danger; both make a suggestion of adoption as a gift; both address the reader directly; both use emotive language (*calamaties, monstrous*).

Identifying the purpose of a text (page 66)

B. Form: advertisement; written to persuade; audience: general public, especially animal lovers.

C. Form: toaster instructions; written to instruct; audience: anyone using the toaster.

D. Form: advertisement; written to persuade; audience: parents who might return to nursing.

E. Form: letter; written to respond to a letter of complaint; audience: a customer who has complained.

How information is presented (page 68)

1. 3 different typefaces are used.
2. Type size varies to draw attention to different pieces of text.
3. Picture of the children makes reader want to help; picture of pound coins helps emphasise how little money is needed to help.

Evaluating the language of a text (page 70)

1. emotive language: *peril, decimate, monster, havoc, devastate* and colloquial language: *dumped, dodged, craze, gobble up.*
2. The writer uses various types of language, eg. emotive (*peril, devastate*), colloquial (*gobble up*) to involve the reader. She/he uses factual language to inform the reader (*producing up to 23 eggs a year*). The direct speech at the end of the article also attracts the reader's attention.

Practice exam questions – Reading (page 86)

QUESTION 1

Facts:
- food poisoning is on the increase
- E.coli bacteria have been found on fruit and vegetables as well as meat
- fruit and vegetables have been fertilised with contaminated manure
- E.coli have developed resistance to some antibiotics

Opinions:
- E.coli bacteria have a deadly enemy: Milton fluid
- perhaps that sounds a bit odd, eccentric even
- You'll find Milton hasn't changed the taste
- more like common sense in fact

QUESTION 2

Beat the Bugs:
- number of cases of food poisoning has quadrupled
- 19 people died in Scotland
- London residents were warned to boil tap water
- references could also be made to facts and figures in the article

Advertisement:
- food poisoning is on the increase
- E.coli bacteria have been found on the surface of fruit and vegetables
- these are resistent to some antibiotics

QUESTION 3

Advert:
- compare/contrast use of picture
- large letters in headline
- informal typeface
- dramatic language (*contaminated*)
- dramatic border to draw attention to ad
- variety of type sizes used
- short paragraphs to make large amount of writing more readable
- use of emotive language (*to make matters worse, deadly enemy*)
- use of colloquial/informal language (*make food go off*)
- direct appeal to the reader
- frequent use of word *you*
- use of questions to involve reader
- attitude to reader: helpful and reassuring

Beat the Bugs:
- varied use of type
- some information in box
- separate headings for different information in the article
- dramatic and eye-catching headline, use of alliteration
- article divided into scientific and non-scientific areas
- direct appeal to the reader in use of the word *you*
- informal beginning (*most people know someone*)
- attitude to reader: serious, not patronising, gives relevant information as well as helpful advice

Glossary

This glossary provides a quick and handy reference to some of the terms used in this book. Use it to check you understand the words and that you can use them correctly in your own answers.

Alliteration

repeating vowels or consonants which sound the same at the beginning of words or stressed syllables. *Example: Peter Piper picked a peck of pickled peppers.*

Argument

the meaning a writer wants to convey in a piece of writing.

Assonance

giving the impression that words sound similar by repeating the same or similar vowel sounds with different consonants, or the same or similar consonants with different vowel sounds. *Example: marrows and carrots in furrows.*

Brainstorming

writing down all the various possible meanings and interpretations you can think of after reading a particular piece of writing.

Colloquialism

an informal word, phrase or piece of English you might use when chatting. *Example: saying* spud *instead of* potato.

Context

the text which surrounds a word or phrase. A word may fit with its context or may appear to surprise you and be out of context.

Cross-referencing

reading or writing about the different works of an author or authors to point out similarities in content and/or types of expression.

Dialogue

conversation between characters.

Emotive language

words or phrases which arouse an emotional response in the reader. *Example: the poor, defenceless animals.*

Figure of speech

where the meaning of a particular expression isn't the same as the literal meaning of the words. *Example: she was over the moon with joy.*

Foregrounding/highlighting

when the author begins consecutive sentences or lines of verse with the same words or structure.

Imagery/images

descriptive words or ideas in a piece of writing.

Irony

using language to express the opposite to what you mean or feel.

Metaphor

describing something by saying it is another thing. *Example: he's a wizard at Maths. (C.f. simile)*

Narrative method/style

how the author tells their story through the piece of writing.

Paradox

a statement that appears to contradict itself. *Example: fair is foul and foul is fair.*

Para-rhyme

words which you expect to rhyme when you see them written down which don't rhyme when you say them out loud. *Example: plough and trough.*

Personification

giving things or ideas human characteristics. *Example: the hot fat spat in the pan.*

Propaganda

material which is written or broadcast to persuade the audience to think in a particular way or follow a certain course of action. When the First World War started, for example, the government issued propaganda (leaflets, articles, posters, radio broadcasts, etc.) to persuade everyone to join the war effort.

Prose

a form of writing which is not in verse and which doesn't rhyme. Novels and newspapers are written in prose.

Rhyme

using pairs or groups of words, usually at the end of lines of verse, which have the same or very similar sounds.

Rhyme scheme

used to discuss the way a poem rhymes. Write A to denote the sound of the last word of the first line. If the second line ends with the same sound, write A again. If it's different, write B. Do the same thing with all the lines in the poem. You might find that the rhyme scheme of a poem with three four-line stanzas is AABB, or ABAB, or ABCA, etc.

Rhyming couplet

two consecutive lines of verse which rhyme with each other, and are usually about the same length. If the rhyme scheme of a poem is AABBCC and so on, the poem is written in rhyming couplets.

Rhythm

a term usually applied to poetry, but which can also be used for drama and prose. Rhythm is produced by the stress given to words when they are read aloud. If the stress falls on words at regular intervals, this is called regular rhythm. If the stress falls with no particular pattern, this is called irregular rhythm.

Simile

describing something by saying it is *like* or *as* something else. *Example: I've been working like a dog. (C.f. metaphor)*

Soliloquy

a speech spoken by an actor alone on stage, designed to reveal the character's innermost thoughts and feelings.

Sonnet

a poem containing fourteen lines.

Stanza

a poem is usually divided into lines grouped together called stanzas. Hymn books call them verses, but make sure you use the word *stanza* in poetry.

Symbol

a word which describes one thing, but also stands for something else. Blake's Rose is both a flower and a representation or *symbol* of love. Many poets use their personal symbols again and again.

Texture

the pattern of rhythm and sound in a poem. A piece of material has a texture built up by the threads used to make it and the way it is woven. Poetry has a texture too, made by the words used and the way they are used.

Verse

a term applied to poetic writing, not prose. Note that a verse (singular) is a single line of a poem.

Word association

using words whose meaning can be used to suggest another meaning. The word *red*, for example, means a colour, but it can also suggest danger or a political belief.